More praise for *Nourishing Vegan Every Day* by Amy Lanza . . .

"*Nourishing Vegan Every Day* is exactly what vegan food should be: delicious first, and vegan second. From comforting classics like Minestrone Soup to innovative eats like Banoffee Pie Jars, vegan and nonvegan cooks will find themselves reaching for this cookbook for satisfying whole-food recipes any night of the week."

—Sarah Fennel, founder of Broma Bakery and Foodtography School

"Quick and easy, this book is filled with nourishing meals you'll want to eat every day. With these delicious recipes, Amy truly delivers on the promise of her wonderful debut cookbook's title."

—Best of Vegan®

"Page after page of beautiful, accessible modern vegan recipes."

—Dave and Steve Flynn, founders of
The Happy Pear and authors of *The Veg Box*

Brimming with creative inspiration, how-to projects, and useful information to enrich your everyday life, Quarto.com is a favorite destination for those pursuing their interests and passions.

© 2023 Quarto Publishing Group USA Inc.
Text and Photography © 2023 Amy Lanza

First Published in 2023 by Fair Winds Press, an imprint of The Quarto Group,
100 Cummings Center, Suite 265-D, Beverly, MA 01915, USA.
T (978) 282-9590 F (978) 283-2742 Quarto.com

Fair Winds Press titles are also available at discount for retail, wholesale, promotional, and bulk purchase. For details, contact the Special Sales Manager by email at specialsales@quarto.com or by mail at The Quarto Group, Attn: Special Sales Manager, 100 Cummings Center, Suite 265-D, Beverly, MA 01915, USA.

27 26 25 24 23   1 2 3 4 5

ISBN: 978-0-7603-7758-1

Digital edition published in 2023
eISBN: 978-0-7603-7759-8

Library of Congress Cataloging-in-Publication Data

Names: Lanza, Amy, author.
Title: Nourishing vegan every day : simple, plant-based recipes filled with color and flavor / Amy Lanza, founder of Nourishing Amy.
Description: Beverly, MA : Fair Winds, 2023. | Summary: "Nourishing Vegan Every Day inspires longtime vegans and the vegan-curious alike with vibrant, flavorful, feel-good recipes"-- Provided by publisher.
Identifiers: LCCN 2022038631 (print) | LCCN 2022038632 (ebook) | ISBN 9780760377581 (hardcover) | ISBN 9780760377598 (ebook)
Subjects: LCSH: Vegan cooking. | Vegans. | LCGFT: Cookbooks.
Classification: LCC TX837 .L25 2023 (print) | LCC TX837 (ebook) | DDC 641.5/6362--dc23/eng/20220817
LC record available at https://lccn.loc.gov/2022038631
LC ebook record available at https://lccn.loc.gov/2022038632

Design: Cindy Samargia Laun
Cover Image: Amy Lanza
Page Layout: Cindy Samargia Laun
Photography: Amy Lanza

Printed in China

The information in this book is for educational purposes only. It is not intended to replace the advice of a physician or medical practitioner. Please see your health-care provider before beginning any new health program.

Simple, Plant-Based Recipes Filled with Color and Flavor

NOURISHING VEGAN EVERY DAY

AMY LANZA Founder of *Nourishing Amy*

FAIR WINDS

CONTENTS

1 BREAKFAST

2 BRUNCH

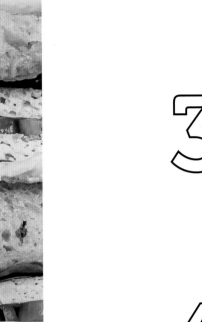

6 SWEETS

7 CELEBRATIONS

INTRODUCTION

I am so excited to bring to you my very first cookbook—something that has been a life-long dream of mine. Thank you for picking it up! I have always been an avid cook and baker, and my passion has only grown stronger over the past few years. Combined with my love for all things plant-based, the kitchen represents my little safe haven: it's my escape from reality, and it's my happy place.

My kitchen is also my place of work (which I am so grateful for). I am the founder of *Nourishing Amy*, where I offer wonderful, unique, plant-based recipes that will tantalize your taste buds with fresh and easy-to-find ingredients. My promise with *Nourishing Amy* is to share *food, health, and happiness.*

I have worked incredibly hard to bring you original, accessible, and delicious recipes on every page of this book. And I hope you will find some brand-new favorites that you'll come back to. Perhaps you'll try something for the first time, or you'll discover a vega-nized variation of your most-loved child-hood dish. Whether you picked up this book to incorporate a few more vegetables and plant-based bakes into your life, or you just love vibrant, soulful, and nourishing food, I hope you find what you're looking for . . . and more. Welcome to my little corner of the cookbook shelf.

WHERE IT ALL BEGAN

Food has been a big part of my life for as long as I remember. Being half-Italian, I have fond memories of bowls of pasta, homemade pastries, and slices of panet-tone. I recall baking mince pies with my Mum every Christmas and sharing big roast dinners with my family on weekends. I truly believe that enjoying food with loved ones promotes togetherness and makes us who we are.

I embarked on my vegan journey while I was studying at university. I began reading food blogs and recipes online that talked about chickpeas and whole grains; tahini and seeds; Medjool dates and frozen banana "ice cream." I was quickly swept up, and I swapped cow's milk for almond milk, chicken for chickpeas, and Greek-style yogurt for creamy coconut yogurt. It was not an overnight switch, but more of a gradual shift in thinking and choices. The more I ate and cooked plant-based, the better I felt: I had more energy. I felt stronger and happier. I had a glow inside of me, and I became enamored with living a life that causes the least amount of harm to others, to animals, and to the planet.

Fast forward five years and the vegan world is abundant with options and meat-free alternatives; although it can seem daunting, and you might not know where to start. This book is about stripping food back to the basics: to relive some of your favorite childhood dishes and enjoy good-for-you, honest meals that happen to be vegan. The recipes are designed so that you won't miss the meat or the dairy. You'll feel satisfied, happy, and *nourished.*

My passion for creating recipes continued to grow, which led me to social media. There, I began to share quick snaps of my dinners and breakfast bowls, and soon I realized there was a demand for vegan recipes with stunning photography to match. So, I worked on my cooking and my flavor combinations, and I studied food photography. I knew my cooking tasted great, but to convince the masses, the food needs to look amazing—I hope you'll feel that way about the recipes in this book.

Nourishing Amy as a Business
I set up *Nourishing Amy* in my mid-twenties; never did I think I'd start my own business, but I knew I wanted to take my social media presence to the next level. I started working with brands and well-known companies to create recipes using their products—and this was called work! But balancing work and pleasure can be difficult, as all self-employed people will understand. Often the lines between work time and playtime become blurred, and it's essential to find some measure of balance every day.

Throughout *Nourishing Vegan Every Day*, you will find recipes using whole-food ingredients and recipes that call for vegan butter, sugar, and white flour. No food is "bad" food, as long as you feel good about your choices and yourself. *Nourishing Amy* is a testament to living your best life.

This is my definition of a nourished lifestyle: when your food makes you feel your best and you listen to your body's cravings. After all, *Nourishing Amy* promotes food, health, and happiness. This is not a diet approach; nor do I promote exclusively eating "healthy" foods. I believe that everything in life is to be enjoyed in moderation: kale salads and chocolate cake.

Skip ahead a few years and the business is flourishing. My work has been shared on the front cover of numerous issues of *Vegan Life* magazine and *PlantBased* magazine, I have been featured in *Thrive Magazine* ,*Vegan Food & Living*, and hosted many live and virtual cooking demos. My photography has been featured online on big-name social media accounts, and I have contributed to recipe cookbooks. I have two self-made e-books, *Nourish Me* and *Nourish Me 2*, and I have an engaged and loyal social media following and a growing email database of subscribers. And finally, I have created the cookbook you hold in your hands.

KEY INGREDIENTS

Here are a few ingredients I cannot live without. I use them a lot throughout the book, so I recommend having them on hand in your kitchen. See the Resources section (page 187) for more details about the brands I use.

The Essentials

I love olive oil, garlic, lemon juice, plant-based milk, thick dairy-free yogurt (e.g., Greek-style or coconut), tamari, nutritional yeast, chia seeds, nut and seed butters, and maple syrup.

Ground Chia or Flaxseed

It is easy to find milled or ground flaxseed in shops, but chia seeds tend to come whole. For smoother batters, I always grind my chia seeds into a fine flour-like texture. Simply add the seeds to a small, high-speed blender and blend to a flour.

Oat Flour

Don't waste money buying oat flour. It is simply oats blended to a flour-like consistency.

Just buy some oats (gluten-free certified if needed). Add them to a blender, process them to a flour-like texture, and store them in a sealed container for up to 2 months.

Coconut Cream

You can buy small pouches or cans of coconut cream, or use a can of full-fat coconut milk. Refrigerate the can for 6 to 8 hours or overnight. Without shaking the can, scoop off the solid part from the top; this is the cream. Save the milky water for smoothies and breakfast oats.

Tofu

I use two main types of tofu: silken tofu and extra-firm tofu. Silken tofu is soft and is great for a creamy texture. Extra-firm tofu has a firm texture and can be sliced and fried off or baked and turned into recipes such as the Almond Satay Tofu Summer Rolls (page 71). If your extra-firm tofu is still a bit soft, place the tofu in a tea towel and top with a plate held down with some cans of beans to squeeze out any excess water.

TOP QUESTIONS ABOUT PLANT-BASED COOKING AND BAKING

Over the years, I've gotten a few questions so many times, and I want to answer them up at the front of this book as well! Hopefully this will save you some time and energy as you tackle the recipes.

Q: How do I replace eggs in vegan cakes and bakes?

There is not one exact answer for replacing eggs, but there are lots of options. For cookies, swap one egg for 1 tablespoon (9 g) of ground chia seeds or flaxseed with 2 to 3 tablespoons (28 to 45 ml) of water. Or use 3 tablespoons (45 ml) of aquafaba (the water from a can of chickpeas). For cakes, it can be slightly more difficult, and it depends on the ratios of fat to liquid and flours, so a lot of the cakes in this book don't use an egg replacer. Instead, we'll rely on "buttermilk" (made from lemon juice and plant-based milk) to bind the batter, and we'll use oil or yogurt to add fat and moisture.

Q: What is aquafaba?

Aquafaba is the water from a can of chickpeas and is an amazing ingredient. Next time you drain a can of chickpeas, save the water or brine to use as egg replacers in cookies.

Q: How can I replace milk and butter?

Thankfully, we have so many options to swap dairy milk, butter, and yogurts too. The same can be said for vegan cheese, ice cream, custards, and creams. Simply choose your favorite dairy-free alternative, such as oat milk, and a block of plant-based butter. Use them where you'd normally use dairy options.

Q: How do I cook tofu so it's not bland and boring?

Tofu can get a bad reputation for being flavorless—that's because it comes plain. For cubes and chunks, slice extra-firm tofu in bite-size pieces and fry it off in olive oil until crispy. Add any seasoning you prefer, such as hot smoked paprika, turmeric, or cumin. Other important seasonings include nutritional yeast, salt and pepper, and kala namak (also known as black salt). Kala namak adds an eggy taste to dishes. A little goes a long way, so I recommend buying a pot to elevate your vegan eggs. It will last you for years.

EQUIPMENT CHECKLIST

I have tried to keep all the recipes basic and accessible throughout the book. Here are a few items of kitchenware and equipment that you'll find useful:

- Kitchen scale: I highly advise using a scale for the most accurate and best results
- Baking pans and trays, such as round tins, loaf pans, and square tins
- Baking parchment and silicone mats (mats are great for multiple uses)
- Mixing bowls and jars
- Spatulas and whisks
- Nonstick frying pans
- Handheld electric mixer
- Food processor for chopping, grating, and slicing
- Blenders are best for smoothies and hummus
- Stand mixer (not essential)
- Waffle maker (not essential)

APPENDIX: CONVERSIONS

Here are few American-English conversions just to be sure!

Food
zucchini: courgette
eggplant: aubergine
cilantro: coriander
arugula: rocket
baking soda: bicarbonate of soda
confectioners' sugar: icing sugar
chile flakes: chilli flakes

Key Cup Conversions
These are a few essential conversions that I stick to throughout the book.

1 cup all-purpose flour = 140 g
1 cup oats = 100 g
1 cup oat flour = 100 g
1 cup nut or seed butter = 240 g
1 cup thick, dairy-free yogurt = 240 g
¼ cup vegan butter = 56 g

1
BREAKFAST

Rise and Shine! Welcome to my breakfast table full of recipes to get your day off to a wonderful start. Whether you are looking for something light and fresh or something more filling and wholesome, this chapter has it all. And all the recipes have been created with ease and speed in mind.

Vibrant smoothies await you from Green Glow to Peanut Butter Protein to Black Forest Gateau (page 17). Slurp and sip one alongside hearty Black Bean and Smashed Avocado Breakfast Burritos (page 35) or Smashed Peas on Toast with Garlicky Mushrooms (page 27).

This chapter also offers a few family favorites easily made vegan with a nourishing twist. Remember toaster pastries? Well, now you can make your own with my healthier Peanut Butter and Raspberry Jam Toaster Pastries (page 21). They taste even better than you remember. What makes this chapter so special to me is that while these are created for breakfast-time, I enjoy these meals at any time of day. Some days nothing beats oatmeal for dinner.

THREE NOURISHING BREAKFAST SMOOTHIES

Serves: 1 | Time: 5 minutes

Smoothies are a great way to pack a few portions of fruits (and vegetables) into your morning with minimal effort. I turn to these three again and again. The Green Glow feels like sunshine and health in every sip; the Peanut Butter Protein tastes like eating peanut butter from the jar; and the Black Forest Gateau tastes like dessert for breakfast. Pick and choose depending on your mood, and slurp away.

For the Green Glow
- 1 banana, chopped and frozen
- ½ zucchini, chopped and frozen (½ cup, or 80 g)
- ½ cup (80 g) frozen mango or pineapple cubes
- ½-inch (1-cm) piece fresh ginger, peeled
- 1 packed cup (30 g) baby spinach
- 1 tablespoon (16 g) almond butter
- 1 tablespoon (15 g) coconut yogurt, plus extra to serve
- ½–¾ cup (120–180 ml) plant-based milk
- ¼ cup (30 g) vegan vanilla protein powder (optional)

To Serve
- ¼ teaspoon chia seeds

For the Peanut Butter Protein
- 1 banana, chopped and frozen
- ½ zucchini, chopped and frozen (½ cup, or 80 g)
- 1 pitted Medjool date or 1 tablespoon (15 ml) maple syrup
- 2 tablespoons (32 g) peanut butter, plus extra to serve
- 1 tablespoon (7 g) hemp seeds
- 1 tablespoon (11 g) chia seeds
- ¼ cup (30 g) vegan vanilla protein powder (optional)
- ¾–1 cup (180–240 ml) plant-based milk

To Serve
- ½ teaspoon crushed peanuts
- 1 teaspoon cacao nibs

For the Black Forest Gateau
- 1 banana, chopped and frozen
- ½ cup (80 g) frozen cherries
- ½ cup (80 g) frozen strawberries or raspberries
- 1 tablespoon (5 g) cacao powder
- 1 tablespoon (15 g) coconut yogurt, plus extra for topping
- ¼ cup (30 g) vegan chocolate protein powder (optional)
- ½–¾ cup (120–180 ml) plant-based milk

To Serve
- 1 teaspoon chopped chocolate
- 1–2 fresh cherries

1. Add all the main smoothie ingredients to a blender. Process until smooth and creamy. Add more milk for a runnier smoothie; use less for a thicker smoothie.
2. Serve with the toppings, and enjoy right away.

SERVING SUGGESTIONS AND VARIATIONS
Turn any of these into a smoothie bowl by using less liquid.

EASY VEGAN OVERNIGHT OATS (THREE WAYS)

Serves: 2 | Time: 10 minutes plus overnight soaking

These are the creamiest and best overnight oats I've made—and they are so easy. They take five to ten minutes to prepare, and breakfast is ready when you wake up in the morning. Choose any of the three variations here, or make this recipe with your favorite flavors. The oats will keep for two to three days in the fridge so they are a great choice for meal prep and for on-the-go breakfasts.

For the Overnight Oat Base

- 1 cup (100 g) oats
- 2 tablespoons (22 g) chia seeds
- ½ cup (120 g) coconut or another thick, dairy-free yogurt
- 1–1½ cups (240 –360 ml) plant-based milk
- 1 teaspoon vanilla extract

For the Strawberries-and-Cream

- 1 cup (160 g) chopped straw-berries, plus extra to serve
- 2–4 tablespoons (30–60 g) coconut yogurt

For the Mocha Caramel

- 2 tablespoons (11 g) cacao powder
- 2 teaspoons (4 g) espresso powder or 2 shots of cooled espresso
- 2 tablespoons (30 ml) maple syrup, divided
- 3 tablespoons (48 g) peanut butter
- A pinch of salt
- 2–4 tablespoons (30–60 g) coconut yogurt
- 1 tablespoon (9 g) chopped peanuts
- 1 tablespoon (5 g) coffee beans, for decoration

STRAWBERRIES-AND-CREAM OATS

1. In a mason jar, stir together all the base ingredients. Start with 1 cup (240 ml) of milk; add more, as needed. Gently stir in the strawberries.
2. Cover and leave overnight in the fridge.
3. Serve the oats layered with yogurt in two jars. Top with more strawberries.

MOCHA CARAMEL OATS

1. In a mason jar, stir together all the base ingredients with the cacao powder, espresso powder, or cooled espresso, and 1 tablespoon (15 ml) of maple syrup. Start with 1 cup (240 ml) of milk; add more as needed.
2. Cover and leave overnight in the fridge.
3. To make the caramel sauce: In a small bowl, stir together the peanut butter, 1 tablespoon (15 ml) of maple syrup, and salt.
4. Serve the oats layered with yogurt and caramel sauce in two jars. Top with some peanuts and coffee beans.

(CONTINUED ON PAGE 20)

(CONTINUED FROM PAGE 19)

For the Chocolate Coconut

- 2 tablespoons (10 g) dried coconut
- 2 tablespoons (22 g) cacao nibs, plus extra to serve
- 3 tablespoons (48 g) peanut butter
- 1 tablespoon (15 ml) maple syrup
- 1 teaspoon cocoa powder
- A pinch of salt
- 2–4 tablespoons (30–60 g) coconut yogurt
- 1 tablespoon (4 g) coconut flakes

CHOCOLATE COCONUT OATS

1. In a mason jar, stir together all the base ingredients with the dried coconut and cacao nibs. Start with 1 cup (240 ml) of milk; add more as needed.
2. Cover and leave overnight in the fridge.
3. To make the chocolate sauce: In a small bowl, stir together the peanut butter, maple syrup, cocoa powder, and salt until smooth and sticky.
4. Serve the oats in two jars layered with yogurt and chocolate sauce. Top with flaked coconut and extra cacao nibs.

PEANUT BUTTER AND RASPBERRY JAM TOASTER PASTRY

Serves: 5 | Time: 40 minutes

These toaster pastries have had the ultimate vegan and healthy makeover with a lightened-up pastry dough, a homemade raspberry jam and peanut butter filling, and a fresh fruit glaze. With a crispy, flaky, golden pastry and a sweet middle, they taste just as good as you remember—if not better! You can play around and try other berries, too.

For the Filling
- 1 heaped cup (125 g) fresh raspberries
- 1 tablespoon (11 g) chia seeds
- 1–2 tablespoons (16–32 g) peanut butter

For the Pastry
- 1 cup (140 g) all-purpose or gluten-free flour, plus extra
- 1 teaspoon baking powder
- ¼ cup (60 g) thick, dairy-free yogurt
- ¼ cup (60 ml) olive or sunflower oil
- 1 teaspoon vanilla extract
- A pinch of salt
- 1 tablespoon (15 ml) plant-based milk

For the Frosting
- ⅜ cup (60 g) confectioners' sugar
- Crushed pistachios (optional)

1. To make the filling: Mash the raspberries with a fork until smooth; small chunks are okay. Stir in the chia seeds. Set it aside while you make the pastry.
2. To make the pastry: Add the flour and baking powder to a large bowl and stir. Pour in the yogurt, olive oil, vanilla, and salt. Stir to a wet and smooth dough, making sure there are no specks of flour. Bring to a ball with your hands, wrap in plastic wrap, and chill for 15 minutes in the fridge.
3. Preheat the oven to 350°F (180°C, or gas mark 4). Line a baking sheet with parchment paper.
4. Once the dough has chilled, lightly dust a surface with flour. Place the dough in the middle and a sheet of parchment paper on top. Roll out the dough with a rolling pin to a rectangle ¼-inch (½-cm) thick. Trim the edges to 10 x 8 inches (26 x 20 cm).
5. Use a ruler to divide the pastry into eight smaller rectangles. Mine measure 2.5 x 4 inches (6 x 10 cm); it does not matter if your size varies from this, as long as they are all the same. Re-roll the pastry to make two more rectangles; you now have ten.
6. Place five pastry rectangles on the baking sheet. Spread with ½ to 1 teaspoon of peanut butter, leaving a gap all around the edges. Top with 1 teaspoon of the raspberry chia jam; you will have some jam left. Carefully place the remaining pastry on top of the fillings and use a fork to crimp all around the edges, pressing fairly firmly. Make three small cuts in the top with a knife to allow any steam to escape.
7. Brush with the milk. Bake for 17 to 20 minutes, or until golden and crisp. Turn the tray around halfway through baking to ensure they cook evenly.

(CONTINUED ON PAGE 23)

(CONTINUED FROM PAGE 21)

8. Allow to cool fully. They will be delicate straight from the oven.

9. Once cool, stir together the confectioners' sugar and 1 tablespoon (20 g) of the raspberry jam until thick. Spread over the pastries and sprinkle on some crushed pistachios (if using). Eat right away, or store leftovers in a sealed container in the fridge for 2 to 3 days. These will freeze for 1 month and defrost at room temperature. To warm them up, place in a warm oven for 5 minutes.

SERVING SUGGESTIONS AND VARIATIONS

The gluten-free pastry is delicious but much more delicate, so be gentle when handling it.

SPICED ALMOND BUTTER OATMEAL WITH STICKY APPLES

Serves: 2 | Time: 20 minutes

Sticky cinnamon apples are delicious on top of thick and creamy apple oatmeal. This one is loaded with almond butter and warming spices such as cinnamon, ginger, and cardamom. Make a batch of this oatmeal for a delicious breakfast that will keep you nourished all morning long.

For the Sticky Apples
- 1 teaspoon coconut oil
- 1 apple, cored and chopped
- 1 teaspoon maple syrup
- ¼ teaspoon ground cinnamon

For the Oatmeal
- 1 cup (100 g) oats
- 1 apple, grated
- 1 tablespoon (11 g) chia seeds
- ½ teaspoon vanilla extract
- 1¾-2 cups (420–480 ml) plant-based milk
- 1 tablespoon (16 g) almond butter
- 1 teaspoon ground cinnamon
- ¼ teaspoon ground ginger
- ¼ teaspoon ground cardamom
- A pinch of salt

To Serve
- 2 tablespoons (30 g) coconut yogurt
- 2 tablespoons (32 g) almond butter
- 1 tablespoon (15 ml) maple syrup
- 1 teaspoon cacao nibs
- 1 teaspoon chia seeds
- 1 teaspoon chopped almonds

1. To make the sticky apples: Heat the coconut oil in a small frying pan over medium-high heat. Once hot, add the apple and cook for 5 minutes, until softening. Pour over the maple syrup and add the cinnamon. Cook for 5 to 10 minutes, until they are soft and sticky.
2. Meanwhile, make the oatmeal: Add all the ingredients to a medium saucepan; start with 1¾ cups (420 ml) of milk. Stir well. Bring to a gentle simmer and cook for 5 to 10 minutes, until thick and creamy. Add more, as needed, for your desired consistency.
3. Divide the oatmeal between two bowls, top with the yogurt, then the sticky apples. Drizzle over the almond butter and maple syrup. Sprinkle with the cacao nibs, chia seeds, and almonds. Eat right away. Once cool, leftover oatmeal will keep in the fridge for 1 to 2 days.

SERVING SUGGESTIONS AND VARIATIONS
For a nut-free version, use tahini and seeds instead of the almond butter and almonds.

SMASHED PEAS ON TOAST WITH GARLICKY MUSHROOMS

Serves: 4 | Time: 20 minutes

As much as I love smashed avocado on toast, sometimes you want a change and these smashed peas really hit the spot. Flavored with garlic and lemon, the chunky pea mix is light and fragrant, and it makes a delicious base for the juiciest garlicky mushrooms. These peas are also great spread onto the Cheesy Broccoli Waffles (page 39) and for serving with Two-Ingredient Flatbreads (page 121).

For the Peas
- 2 cups (300 g) peas, thawed
- 2 tablespoons (12 g) chopped fresh mint
- 1½ tablespoons (25 ml) lemon juice
- 2 tablespoons (15 g) tahini
- 1½ tablespoons (25 ml) olive oil
- 1–2 cloves garlic, crushed
- ½ lemon, zested
- Salt and pepper, to taste

For the Mushrooms
- 14 ounces (400 g) mushrooms
- 1 tablespoon (15 ml) olive oil
- 6 cloves garlic, crushed
- Salt and pepper, to taste

To Serve
- 4 large or 8 small slices of bread
- Fresh mint leaves, chopped
- Homemade Dukkah (page 97)

1. To make the smashed peas: Add all the ingredients to a food processor or blender, reserving a few peas for topping. Blend to a chunky mix. I like to keep some small chunks of peas, but make it as smooth as you like. Season with salt and pepper. This can be made ahead of time and stored in a sealed container for 3 to 5 days in the fridge.
2. To make the mushrooms: If using button mushrooms, leave them whole or slice in half. Slice larger mushrooms into strips. Heat the olive oil in a large pan over medium-high heat. Once hot, add the mushrooms, garlic, salt, and pepper. Fry for about 10 minutes, until really juicy and starting to turn golden.
3. Toast the bread and spread with the smashed peas. Top with the garlicky mushrooms, mint, dukkah, and the reserved peas.

SERVING SUGGESTIONS AND VARIATIONS
Make sure to use gluten-free bread where needed.

PEACHES-AND-CREAM BAKED OATS

Serves: 4 | Time: 40 minutes

If you fancy cake for breakfast, then these baked oats are the answer. They are light, fluffy, and tender like a cake, but they are made with delicious plant-based and nourishing ingredients. With thick, dairy-free yogurt and slices of sticky peach, these oats are great warm or cold and what's even better is that you can make and bake them in one dish!

For the Oats

- 1 ripe banana
- ½ cup (120 g) thick, dairy-free yogurt
- ½ cup (120 ml) plant-based milk
- 2 tablespoons (30 ml) plus 1 teaspoon (5 ml) maple syrup, divided
- 1 teaspoon vanilla extract
- 1 cup (100 g) oats
- 1 tablespoon (11 g) chia seeds
- ¼ cup (15 g) coconut flakes
- 1 teaspoon baking powder
- 1 peach, sliced

To Serve

- 2–4 tablespoons (30–60 g) thick, dairy-free yogurt
- Toasted coconut flakes
- Extra maple syrup

1. Preheat the oven to 350°F (180°C, or gas mark 4), and have an 8-inch (20-cm) round dish to hand.
2. Mash the banana directly into the dish until smooth. Stir in the yogurt, milk, 2 tablespoons (30 ml) of maple syrup, and vanilla until smooth.
3. Pour in the oats, chia seeds, coconut flakes, and baking powder and stir until combined and thick.
4. Slice the peach and arrange the slices on top of the oats, pressing them down slightly. Brush the fruits with 1 teaspoon (5 ml) of maple syrup (this prevents them drying out and will become sticky once baked).
5. Bake for 32 to 35 minutes, until golden and crisping at the edges and slightly tender in the middle.
6. Allow to cool for 5 minutes. Enjoy these warm or cold, with some yogurt, toasted coconut flakes, and maple syrup. To warm up the oats, place them in the oven at 350°F (180°C, or gas mark 4), for 5 to 10 minutes. Once cool, store the baked oats in a sealed container in the fridge for 2 to 3 days or in the freezer for up to 1 month. Defrost at room temperature.

SERVING SUGGESTIONS AND VARIATIONS

Try these baked oats with other fruits such as sliced plums, nectarines, or apples, too.

COOKIE-LOVER'S SMOOTHIE BOWL

Serves: 1 | Time: 15 minutes

This smoothie bowl will surprise you: it tastes just like a thick vanilla shake, but it's secretly loaded with fruits and vegetables. Maybe you don't notice because it is topped with the best (and easiest) edible cookie dough. I make this smoothie bowl all the time in the summer when I fancy cookie dough and milkshakes in the morning—it really will make you smile from the inside out.

For the Cookie Dough
- 2 tablespoons (30 g) peanut butter
- 1 tablespoon (15 ml) maple syrup
- ½ teaspoon vanilla extract
- ¼ cup (25 g) oat flour
- A pinch of salt
- 1 ounces (25 g) dairy-free chocolate chips

For the Smoothie Bowl
- 1 banana, chopped and frozen
- ½ avocado, chopped and frozen
- ½ zucchini, chopped and frozen (½ cup, or 80 g)
- ¼ cup (30 g) frozen blueberries
- ½–1 teaspoon blue spirulina powder
- ½ teaspoon vanilla extract
- ¼ cup (30 g) vegan vanilla protein powder (optional)
- ⅔–1 cup (160–240 ml) plant-based milk
- 1 tablespoon (15 g) coconut yogurt
- 1 tablespoon (11 g) cacao nibs
- 1 teaspoon chia seeds

1. To make the cookie dough: In a small bowl, stir together the peanut butter, maple syrup, and vanilla until smooth. Pour in the oat flour and salt, stir to a sticky dough, then fold in the chocolate chips. Roll the dough into small balls. Chill in the fridge for 10 minutes.
2. To make the smoothie bowl: Add the banana, avocado, zucchini, blueberries, blue spirulina, vanilla, protein powder (if using) and ⅔ cup (160 ml) of plant-based milk to a blender; a high-speed blender works best. Blend until really smooth, adding more milk as needed. I like to keep it thick like ice cream, but you can make it runnier with more milk.
3. Pour the smoothie into a bowl. Top with the yogurt, cacao nibs, and chai seeds. Top with the cookie dough balls. Eat right away, and store any extra cookie dough in the fridge for up 1 to week.

SERVING SUGGESTIONS AND VARIATIONS
If you can't find blue spirulina powder, leave it out; the smoothie will be more green-blue in color.

CHOCOLATE, PEANUT BUTTER, AND BANANA BREAKFAST COOKIES

Serves: 20 | Time: 20 minutes

Cookies for breakfast? Yes, please! Especially when they combine three of my favorite things: chocolate, peanut butter, and banana. These cookies are made from everyday breakfast staples—meaning you really can have your cookies all day long. These are made from just seven ingredients and are ready in twenty minutes. Plus, you can swap the peanuts and chocolate chips for other add-ins such as hazelnuts, raisins, macadamia nuts, seeds . . . the possibilities are endless.

For the Cookies

- 2 tablespoons (18 g) ground chia or flaxseed, plus 5 tablespoons (74 ml) water
- 1 banana, mashed
- ¾ cup (180 g) smooth, runny peanut butter
- 2 teaspoons (10 ml) vanilla extract
- 2 cups (200 g) oats
- 1 teaspoon baking powder
- A pinch of salt
- ½ cup (80 g) dairy-free chocolate chips
- ½ cup (60 g) peanuts, chopped

1. Preheat the oven to 350°F (180°C, or gas mark 4). Line a baking sheet with parchment paper. Optional step: To roast the peanuts (it adds a lot of flavor), add the peanuts to the tray and roast for 10 minutes. Cool fully, then roughly chop, and set the peanuts aside.
2. Stir together the chia seeds and water. Set aside for 5 minutes to form a gel.
3. Add the banana to a large mixing bowl. Stir in the peanut butter, vanilla, and chia gel until smooth.
4. Pour in the oats, baking powder, and salt. Stir to a thick, sticky cookie dough.
5. Fold in the chocolate chips and peanuts. Divide into twenty small balls (2 tablespoons, or 35 grams each).
6. Flatten each ball onto the baking sheet as these cookies do not spread.
7. Bake for 12 minutes, or until golden and crisp at the edges. I like to turn the tray halfway through to ensure they all cook evenly.
8. Cool for 10 minutes and enjoy, or allow the cookies to cool fully on a wire rack. Store the cookies in a sealed container at room temperature for 3 to 5 days, in the fridge for 1 week, or freeze the cookies for up to 1 month.

SERVING SUGGESTIONS AND VARIATIONS

- *Play around with the flavors, add ½ cup (60 g) seeds or dried fruits instead of the peanuts.*
- *Make these nut-free by using a seed butter, such as tahini, and seeds instead of peanut butter and peanuts.*

BLACK BEAN AND SMASHED AVOCADO BREAKFAST BURRITOS

Serves: 4 | Time: 25 minutes

This breakfast is great for busy mornings when you need a filling but wholesome meal to start the day. Ready in twenty-five minutes, make up a quick spiced, tomatoey black bean filling, then stuff it inside tortilla wraps alongside some fresh spinach and lime-infused smashed avocado. I like to enjoy these burritos with a cold juice or Green Glow Smoothie (page 17).

For the Black Beans
- 1 tablespoon (15 ml) olive oil
- 1 red onion, small dice
- 1 red bell pepper, small dice
- 2 large cloves garlic, crushed
- ½ teaspoon hot smoked paprika
- ½ teaspoon ground cumin
- A pinch of chile flakes
- 1 can black beans (drained: 8½ ounces, or 240 g)
- 1 heaping cup (170 g) cherry tomatoes, halved
- Salt and pepper, to taste

To Serve
- 2 avocados
- 2 tablespoons (28 ml) lime juice
- 2 scallions, thinly sliced
- 2 tablespoons (2 g) chopped fresh cilantro
- Salt and pepper, to taste
- 4 tortilla wraps
- 1 heaped cup (40 g) baby spinach

1. To make the black beans: Heat the olive oil in a medium frying pan. Once hot, add the onion, bell pepper, and garlic. Fry for 10 minutes over medium-high heat until softening.
2. Add the hot smoked paprika, cumin, and chile flakes, and fry for 1 minute. Add the black beans, tomatoes, salt, and pepper. Cook for 10 minutes, stirring frequently to prevent the beans from sticking to the pan. As they cook, feel free to mash the beans and tomatoes slightly with a wooden spoon.
3. To make the smashed avocado: Peel and de-stone the avocados, then mash it with a fork. Add the lime juice, scallions, cilantro, salt, and pepper.
4. To make the burritos: Place a tortilla down and add some spinach into the middle. Top with one-quarter of the smashed avocado and one-quarter of the beans. Fold in the sides as you wrap side of the tortilla closest to you up and over the filling and continue to roll to seal in the edges.
5. Slice in half and enjoy right away. Leftover black bean filling will keep in a sealed container for 2 to 3 days in the fridge, and the avocado will keep for 1 to 2 days. These are best wrapped when you are ready to eat as the tortillas can soften over time.

SERVING SUGGESTIONS AND VARIATIONS
Try these burritos with other beans or pulses, such as lentils, chickpeas, or kidney beans.

2

BRUNCH

Picture this: it's the weekend and you have no other plans than to make the best plant-based brunch. This is the chapter for you. Filled with sweet recipes and savory options, recipes that take a little more time and those ready in less than thirty minutes. All of these brunch dishes will make for the happiest midmorning meal.

And this chapter isn't only for weekends! The recipes are delicious any day of the week and at any time. I think the best thing about brunch is that anything goes (that's why it is my favorite meal of the day). I love to dive into a plate of Cheesy Broccoli Waffles (page 39) for dinner. When a sweet tooth strikes, nothing beats a tall stack of fluffy Oat Blender-Pancakes (page 55) with three flavor options: vanilla berry, chocolate coconut, or espresso cinnamon. Bake up a loaf of Muesli Banana Bread (page 49) or some No Yeast Sticky Pecan Buns (page 51), or impress your guests with Vegan Eggs Benedict with Homemade Hollandaise and Mushroom "Bacon" (page 41).

CHEESY BROCCOLI WAFFLES

Serves: 4 to 5 | Time: 30 minutes

These cheesy waffles really are a game changer for brunch. Even those that are on the fence about broccoli are likely to love these thanks to the light, fluffy waffle batter, the tasty dairy-free cheese, and the crispy golden outside. We like to serve these with a quick "sour cream" (lemony yogurt), avocado, and some greens.

For the Waffles
- 2¾–3 cups (200 g) broccoli (florets and small stems)
- 1 cup (140 g) all-purpose or gluten-free flour
- 1 cup (100 g) chickpea/gram flour
- 2 teaspoons (9 g) baking powder
- 1 teaspoon hot smoked paprika
- 1 teaspoon garlic granules
- ¼ cup (20 g) nutritional yeast
- 2 cups (480 ml) unsweetened plant-based milk
- ⅔ cup (80 g) grated dairy-free cheese
- Salt and pepper, to taste
- Oil, for the waffle iron

For Topping
- ½ cup (120 g) thick, unsweetened, dairy-free yogurt
- 1 tablespoon (15 ml) lemon juice
- 2 avocados, peeled and sliced
- 2 handfuls arugula
- Fresh parsley or cilantro
- A pinch of chile flakes

1. Chop the broccoli very small. Grate it, or add it to a food processor and blitz until it's very small.
2. To make the waffle batter: Sift the flours into a large mixing bowl. Add the baking powder, hot smoked paprika, garlic granules, and nutritional yeast. Whisk to mix.
3. Pour in the milk and whisk until almost fully combined. Add the grated cheese and broccoli. Stir to combine the batter, and season with salt and pepper.
4. Let the batter rest while you heat the waffle iron. You will be making waffles in batches; to keep them warm set the oven to a very low temperature or have a covered plate ready.
5. Once the iron is hot, brush or spray with oil. Add around ⅓ to ½ cup (a few tablespoons) of batter per waffle; the amount will depend on the size of your waffle maker. Cook the waffles according to your waffle iron instructions, until golden and crisp outside. I like to wait until most of the steam has gone which is always longer than the machine says.
6. When the waffles are finished, keep them warm. Repeat to make 8 to 10 waffles.
7. To make the toppings: In a small bowl, stir together the yogurt and lemon juice with a pinch of salt. Peel, de-stone, and slice the avocado.
8. Serve the waffles warm topped with the lemon yogurt, avocado, arugula, herbs, and chile flakes.
9. Leftover waffles will keep in a sealed container for 2 to 3 days in the fridge or up to 1 month in the freezer. Warm them back up in the oven, in a hot pan, or in a toaster.

SERVING SUGGESTIONS AND VARIATIONS
If you don't have a waffle iron, make these into pancakes by cooking them in a greased nonstick frying pan and flipping over once golden and cooked through.

VEGAN EGGS BENEDICT WITH HOMEMADE HOLLANDAISE AND MUSHROOM "BACON"

Serves: 4 | Time: 30 minutes

The ultimate veganized breakfast favorite: eggs Benedict like you have never seen them before. A lightly toasted muffin topped with smoky, spicy, sticky-sweet mushroom "bacon," a deliciously tender tofu "egg," fresh avocado, and the quickest and creamiest vegan hollandaise sauce. These eggs Benedict really are a Sunday brunch staple.

For the Hollandaise
- 8 ounces (220 g) silken tofu
- 2 tablespoons (28 ml) lemon juice
- 2 tablespoons (28 ml) melted vegan butter
- 2 tablespoons (10 g) nutritional yeast
- ½ teaspoon Dijon mustard
- ¼ teaspoon cayenne pepper
- ¼ teaspoon ground turmeric
- ¼ teaspoon kala namak (optional)
- Salt and pepper, to taste

For the Mushroom "Bacon"
- 4 large portobello mushrooms
- 2 tablespoons (30 ml) olive oil
- 2 tablespoons (30 ml) maple syrup
- ¼ cup (60 ml) tamari
- ¾–1 teaspoon hot smoked paprika
- 1 teaspoon garlic granules or 1 garlic clove
- 2 teaspoons (10 g) miso paste

For the Tofu "Eggs"
- 14 ounces (400 g) extra-firm tofu
- 1 tablespoon (5 g) nutritional yeast
- ¼ teaspoon garlic granules
- ¼ teaspoon kala namak (optional)
- Salt and pepper, to taste
- 1–2 tablespoons (15–30 ml) olive oil, for frying

To Serve
- 4 English muffins
- 1 avocado, peeled and sliced
- 1 tablespoon (4 g) chopped fresh parsley or cilantro
- ¼ teaspoon chile flakes
- Fresh tomatoes

1. To make the hollandaise sauce: Add everything to a blender and process until really smooth. Pour into a saucepan and warm through to thicken the sauce; if it starts to thicken too much, add 2 to 4 tablespoons (28 to 60 ml) of water. Serve warm, or cool and store in the fridge for 2 to 3 days in a sealed jar. Warm back up on the stove with a splash of water.

2. To make the mushroom "bacon": Preheat the oven to 400°F (200°C, or gas mark 6). Line a large tray with parchment paper. Slice the mushrooms into ½-inch (1-cm) strips. Whisk together the remaining marinade ingredients, and season it with salt and pepper. Toss the mushrooms in the marinade and leave for 5 to 30 minutes. Transfer the mushrooms to the tray and bake for 10 minutes. Flip each slice and bake for 5 minutes until juicy, tender, and starting to crisp at the edges.

(CONTINUED ON PAGE 42)

(CONTINUED FROM PAGE 41)

3. To make the tofu "eggs": Slice the tofu block so that you can cut out four circles that are just smaller than the size of your English muffins. Save the rest of the tofu for other recipes. Or, slice the tofu into squares. Add the nutritional yeast, garlic granules, and kala namak (if using) to a shallow bowl with some salt and pepper. Coat each piece of tofu; this flavors the tofu.

4. Heat a large, nonstick, frying pan over medium-high heat. Heat the oil and fry each tofu "egg" for about 3 to 5 minutes on each side, until golden brown on both sides.

5. To assemble: Halve and toast the muffins. Top each half of muffin with some of the mushroom "bacon" and then a tofu "egg." Add some avocado, and pour over the hollandaise sauce. Add some herbs and chile flakes. Serve with fresh tomatoes.

SERVING SUGGESTIONS AND VARIATIONS

The mushroom "bacon" is delicious on its own and is great for adding to Nourish Bowls (page 94).

SWEET POTATO CARROT FRITTERS WITH AVOCADO SALSA

Serves: 4 (makes 12 fritters) | Time: 30 minutes

Perfect for a savory brunch, these vegetable fritters are quick and easy to come together, and they only use one pan. They are packed with warming flavors, golden and crisp on the outside, but tender and soft on the inside. My friends and I also love these as a quick snack, light lunch, or as part of a grazing dinner.

For the Fritters
- 2 large sweet potatoes
- 2 large carrots
- 1–2 tablespoons (15–30 ml) olive oil, plus extra for frying
- 4 scallions, sliced small
- 4 cloves garlic, crushed
- ¼ cup (10 g) chopped fresh parsley or cilantro
- 1 teaspoon ground cumin
- A pinch of chile flakes
- Salt and pepper, to taste
- 4 cups (100 g) chopped baby spinach
- ¼ cup (20 g) nutritional yeast
- 2 tablespoons (28 ml) tamari
- ½–¾ cup (70–105 g) gluten-free or all-purpose flour

For the Salsa
- 2 avocados
- 1 heaping cup (170 g) cherry tomatoes
- 2 tablespoons (8 g) chopped fresh parsley or cilantro
- 2 tablespoons (28 ml) lime juice
- Salt and pepper, to taste

1. Peel and grate the sweet potatoes and measure out 14 ounces (400 g). Peel and grate the carrots and measure out 11 ounces (320 g).
2. Heat a large, nonstick, frying pan with the olive oil over medium-high heat. Add the sweet potato, carrot, scallion, and garlic. You may need to work in two batches. Fry for 5 minutes over medium to high heat, then add the herbs, cumin, chile flakes, salt, and pepper. Toss well and continue to fry for 5 to 10 minutes, until the vegetables are less vibrant and have softened. Add the spinach, and fry for 1 to 2 minutes to wilt.
3. Transfer to a large mixing bowl. Add the nutritional yeast and tamari. Add ½ cup (about 70 g) of flour and stir the mix. Add more flour as needed to reach a sticky mixture; it will be slightly wet but hold together easily into fritters.
4. Divide the mixture into twelve equal pieces and shape into fritters, about 2 inches (or 5 cm in diameter).
5. Clean out the frying pan and add a little more oil. Once hot, place three or four fritters (or as many as you can fit) into the pan. Fry for 3 to 5 minutes, until golden and crisping up. Flip over and cook on the second side. Repeat to cook all twelve fritters.

(CONTINUED ON PAGE 45)

(CONTINUED FROM PAGE 43)

6. To make the salsa: Peel, de-stone, and cut the avocados into small cubes. Slice the tomatoes in half or quarters and add to a small bowl with the avocado. Stir in the herbs and lime juice, and season with salt and pepper. Toss well.

7. Serve the fritters alongside the fresh salsa. Enjoy these fritters warm or cold. Reheat by cooking them in the oven at 350°F (180°C, or gas mark 4) for 5 minutes or reheat in a pan. Once cool, fritters will keep for 2 to 3 days wrapped in the fridge or for up to 1 month in the freezer.

SERVING SUGGESTIONS AND VARIATIONS

These fritters are also delicious served with the smashed peas (page 27).

RED PEPPER AND TOFU "EGG" SHAKSHUKA

Serves: 4 | Time: 45 minutes

Shakshuka has always been one of my favorite brunch dishes, and this recipe really shows off what you can do with plant-based ingredients. These "eggs" are baked into the rich tomato sauce, and they are made from tofu, kala namak for the "eggyness," and turmeric for the "yolk." This is such a crowd-pleasing dish that encourages everyone to dig in and mop up the sauce with fresh bread.

For the Tofu "Egg"
- 7 ounces (200 g) extra-firm tofu
- 2 tablespoons (10 g) nutritional yeast
- ½ teaspoon garlic granules
- ½ teaspoon kala namak (optional)
- 2 tablespoons (12 g) chickpea flour
- ¼ cup (60 ml) plus 2 teaspoons (10 ml) plant-based milk
- Salt and pepper, to taste
- ½ teaspoon ground turmeric

For the Shakshuka
- 1 tablespoon (15 ml) olive oil
- 2 red onions, thinly sliced
- 4 cloves garlic, crushed
- 2 red bell peppers, thinly sliced
- 1 teaspoon hot smoked paprika
- 1½ teaspoons ground cumin
- 2 tablespoons (8 g) chopped fresh parsley
- Salt and pepper, to taste
- 2 cans (14 ounces, or 400 g each) chopped tomatoes
- 2 tablespoons (32 g) tomato paste (purée)

To Serve
- 1 avocado, peeled and sliced
- 2-4 tablespoons (18–36 g) Homemade Dukkah (page 97)
- 1 tablespoon (4 g) chopped fresh parsley or cilantro
- 4-8 slices of bread

1. To make the tofu "egg" mix: Add all the ingredients except the turmeric to a small blender; start with ¼ cup (60 ml) of milk. Process until no lumps remain, and add more milk as needed. Remove 1 tablespoon (about 15 ml) of the mixture. Stir it with the turmeric for the "egg yolk." The egg can be prepared in advance and stored in sealed containers in the fridge for 2 to 3 days.

2. To make the shakshuka: Heat the olive oil in a large frying pan over medium-high heat. Add the onion and garlic and fry for 5 minutes, until softening. Add the bell pepper and fry for 5 minutes. Add the hot smoked paprika, cumin, parsley, salt, and pepper. Fry for 1 minute until you can smell the spices. Pour in the tomatoes and tomato paste, then stir well. Bring to a boil, then reduce the heat to a simmer. Cover with a lid and simmer for 20 minutes.

3. With the shakshuka on the heat, make four wells in the tomatoey mix. Spoon the tofu "egg" in round shapes into the holes and top with the turmeric "egg yolk." Place the lid on and simmer for 5 minutes. Remove the lid and cook for 5 minutes to allow the "egg" to cook through.

4. Top the shakshuka with avocado, herbs, and dukkah, and serve it with the bread.

5. Once cool, keep leftovers in a sealed container in the fridge for 2 to 3 days, or freeze the mixture (without the "egg") for up to 1 month.

SERVING SUGGESTIONS AND VARIATIONS
Instead of the tofu "egg," stir in one can of chickpeas (drained: 8½ ounces, or 240 grams) into the shakshuka along with the tomatoes.

MUESLI BANANA BREAD

Serves: 10 | **Time: 70 minutes plus cooling**

To give a bit of background to this recipe, I have a bit of a banana bread obsession and have been creating a brand-new recipe each month since January 2020—so I simply had to include a banana bread in this book. This is great for brunch: It's light, moist, spongy, and made with whole foods. Packed with berries, fruit, nut muesli, and yogurt, I love a thick slice topped with more yogurt, berries, nut butter, and maple syrup.

For the Banana Bread

- 2 large mashed bananas (1 cup, or 250 g)
- ¼ cup (60 ml) maple syrup
- ¼ cup (35 g) coconut or caster sugar
- ½ cup (120 g) runny, smooth nut or seed butter
- ½ cup (120 ml) plant-based milk
- ½ cup (120 g) thick, dairy-free yogurt
- 1 tablespoon (15 ml) vanilla extract
- ¾ cup (100 g) fresh or frozen blueberries
- 1½ cups (210 g) plus 1 teaspoon all-purpose or gluten-free flour, divided
- 1½ teaspoons baking powder
- ½ teaspoon baking soda
- 1½ teaspoons ground cinnamon
- ½ cup (50 g) plus 1 tablespoon (6 g) muesli, divided
- 1 tablespoon (9 g) ground chia or flaxseed
- A pinch of salt

1. Preheat the oven to 350°F (180°C, or gas mark 4). Line a 9- x 5-inch (23- x 13-cm) loaf pan with parchment paper.
2. Add the banana to a large mixing bowl with the maple syrup, sugar, nut butter, milk, yogurt, and vanilla. Whisk until smooth.
3. Add the blueberries and 1 teaspoon of flour to a small bowl. Toss to combine.
4. Sift the remaining flour, baking powder, baking soda, and cinnamon into the mashed banana mix. Add the ½ cup (50 g) of muesli, ground chia, and salt. Whisk or stir to a thick but smooth batter. Add most of the floured blueberries (leaving any excess flour behind) and stop mixing when no specks of flour remain.
5. Pour the batter into the loaf pan, and smooth over the top. Sprinkle over the 1 tablespoon (6 g) muesli and the remaining blueberries. Press in any dried fruits from the muesli as these will burn in the oven.
6. Bake for 60 minutes, or until an inserted skewer comes out clean. It's normal if there are some specks of cakey batter. Check the loaf after 30 minutes and cover the top with tinfoil to keep it from browning.

(CONTINUED ON PAGE 50)

(CONTINUED FROM PAGE 49)

7. Cool for 10 minutes in the loaf pan, then carefully lift out and cool fully on a wire rack.
8. Once cool, slice and serve. Leftovers will keep in a sealed container in the fridge for 3 to 5 days and in the freezer for up to 1 month.

SERVING SUGGESTIONS AND VARIATIONS

- *Use any nut or seed butter; cashew butter, almond butter, or tahini all work well.*
- *You can make this loaf into 12 muffins and bake them for 22 to 24 minutes.*

NO YEAST STICKY PECAN BUNS

Serves: 12 | Time: 40 minutes plus cooling time

You are going to fall in love with these vegan sticky buns. And the best part is that they contain no yeast. This means no kneading, no proofing, and no waiting around! Simply make the two-ingredient "magic" dough, then spread with a quick homemade salted caramel, and sprinkle with crushed pecans. Roll up and bake until sticky and golden before tearing and sharing these buns one by one.

For the Caramel

- 1½ cups (240 g) light brown sugar
- ½ cup (100 g) coconut cream
- ⅓ cup (80 ml) maple syrup
- 2 heaped teaspoons (6 g) ground cinnamon
- A pinch of salt
- 1½ cups (180 g) pecans, roughly chopped

For the Dough

- 1 cup (240 g) thick, dairy-free yogurt, such as coconut
- 1½ cups (210 g) self-raising flour, plus extra for dusting
- A pinch of salt

1. To make the caramel: Add the sugar, cream, syrup, and cinnamon to a medium saucepan and warm through over high heat. Allow the coconut cream to melt to form a smooth mixture, then bring it to a boil. Whisk continually while the caramel bubbles and cook for 1 minute. Whisk in the salt, and then remove from the heat. Pour into a medium bowl and chill in the fridge for 1 hour, or until thick and glossy. This can be made up to 3 days beforehand and kept in a sealed container in the fridge.
2. Preheat the oven to 350°F (180°C, or gas mark 4). Line a 7- x 9-inch (18- x 23-cm) dish with parchment paper.
3. To make the dough: Add the yogurt and flour to a large bowl with a pinch of salt. Stir to a shaggy dough. Set the dough on a lightly floured surface; I like to use a floured silicone mat. Gently knead for 1 minute with your hands. Roll out the dough to a 14- x 10-inch (36- x 25-cm) rectangle.
4. Pour or spread half of the caramel directly into the dish and cover with half of the pecans. Spread the remaining caramel all over the dough, leaving a small border around the edges. Sprinkle over the remaining pecans.
5. Using the long edge, roll up the dough into a log (like you do for cinnamon rolls). Trim off the ends to leave a 12-inch (30-cm) log. Slice this into twelve rolls.
6. Place the rolls on top of the caramel in the dish, nestled snugly.
7. Bake for 27 to 32 minutes, or until golden on top and cooked through.

(CONTINUED ON PAGE 53)

(CONTINUED FROM PAGE 51)

8. Cool for 10 minutes, then carefully invert the buns onto a plate or serving dish. It is best to do this quickly, so the caramel doesn't harden and stick to the parchment and pan. Don't worry if there is caramel oozing out the sides. Peel off the parchment. Enjoy warm or allow to cool.
9. Store leftovers in a sealed container for 2 to 3 days or in the freezer for up to 1 month (defrost at room temperature).

SERVING SUGGESTIONS AND VARIATIONS

Swap the self-raising flour for a gluten-free self-raising blend; the dough will be slightly more delicate.

FLUFFY OAT BLENDER-PANCAKES

Serves: Serves 4 (makes 12 pancakes) | Time: 20 minutes

These pancakes are hands down the best fluffy pancakes you've ever made in the blender. With banana, oats, and plant-based milk, these are good-for-you pancakes that are so quick and easy to serve up to hungry guests. Try vanilla berry, chocolate coconut, or espresso cinnamon stacks, or experiment with it and play with your favorite flavors and toppings.

For the Basic Pancake
- 1 medium-large ripe banana
- 1½ cups (150 g) oat flour
- 2 teaspoons (9 g) baking powder
- ¾ cup (180 ml) plant-based milk
- 1 tablespoon (15 ml) maple syrup, plus extra to serve
- 1 tablespoon (15 ml) lemon juice
- A pinch of salt
- Oil, for greasing
- 2–4 tablespoons (30–60 g) thick, dairy-free yogurt, to serve
- 2–4 tablespoons (30–60 ml) maple syrup

Vanilla Berry Pancakes
- 1 teaspoon vanilla extract
- 1 cup (140 g) berries, fresh or frozen
- Extra berries

Chocolate Coconut Pancakes
- 1 tablespoon (5 g) cacao powder
- 1–2 tablespoons (15–28 ml) plant-based milk
- ¼ cup (40 g) dairy-free chocolate chips, plus extra to serve
- 2 tablespoons (10 g) dried coconut
- 2 tablespoons (10 g) toasted coconut flakes

Espresso Cinnamon Pancakes
- 1 teaspoon espresso/coffee powder
- 1 teaspoon ground cinnamon, plus extra to serve

1. To make the pancake batter: Add the banana, flour, baking powder, milk, syrup, lemon juice, and salt to a blender. Process until smooth. Leave for 5 minutes to rest.
2. To make the vanilla berry pancakes: Blend the vanilla into the batter. Add a few berries on top of the pancakes as they cook (in step 5).
3. To make the chocolate coconut: Blend the cacao powder into the batter. Add 1 to 2 tablespoons (15 to 28 ml) of milk as needed to reach a smooth consistency. Fold in the chocolate chips and coconut.
4. To make the espresso cinnamon: Add the espresso and cinnamon to the blender.
5. You'll be working in batches; have a covered plate ready or warm the oven. Lightly oil a large, nonstick pan and heat it over medium-high heat. Add 2 tablespoons (30 ml) of pancake batter to the pan per pancake, making a small round shape. Allow the underside to cook and turn golden and slightly crisp, while bubbles will appear on the surface. Once cooked, flip over and cook on the second side until fluffy.
6. Keep the pancakes warm, and repeat to make all twelve pancakes.
7. Serve the pancakes stacked up and topped with yogurt, maple syrup, and any other toppings. Once cool, pancakes will keep for 2 to 3 days in the fridge or can be frozen for up to 1 month. Defrost and warm back them up in a frying pan.

SERVING SUGGESTIONS AND VARIATIONS
- *For the vanilla berry pancakes, any small berry such as blueberries, raspberries, or chopped up strawberries will be delicious.*
- *Make your own oat flour by blitzing oats in a blender to a fine flour-like consistency.*

BANANA-CARAMEL FRENCH TOAST

Serves: 4 | Time: 40 minutes

French toast is a must for brunch, and I like mine fluffy, tender, and golden. This stack is made egg-free by using aquafaba, yogurt, and cornstarch to create a delicious batter. Then top the toast with a quick caramel and slices of banana. Or make it your own by topping these with chocolate chips or fresh strawberries, or keep it simple with maple syrup and dairy-free ice cream.

For the French Toast
- 8 slices of day-old bread
- 1 cup (240 ml) plant-based milk
- ¼ cup (60 ml) aquafaba
- ¼ cup (60 ml) maple syrup
- ¼ cup (60 g) dairy-free yogurt
- 2 teaspoons (6 g) cornstarch or arrowroot powder
- 1 teaspoon vanilla extract
- A pinch of salt
- Oil or vegan butter, for the pan

For the Caramel
- ½ cup (120 g) runny, smooth nut or seed butter
- 2 tablespoons (30 ml) maple syrup
- 2 tablespoons (30 ml) melted coconut oil
- A pinch of salt

To Serve
- ½ cup (120 g) thick dairy-free yogurt
- 2 bananas, sliced
- ½ cup (70 g) fresh blueberries
- ¼ cup (60 ml) maple syrup
- Powdered sugar, to dust

1. To make the French toast: Add all the ingredients apart from the bread and oil to a large, shallow bowl. Whisk until smooth. Dip each slice of bread into the batter; allow both sides to soak up some of the mixture. Leave the soaked bread to rest for 10 minutes. I like to use a shallow bowl and pour any excess batter on top.

2. To make the caramel: Add all the ingredients to a small bowl. Stir together until smooth. Use right away or keep in a sealed container for 3 to 5 days or in the fridge for 1 week. If it firms up, simply warm it back up.

3. Heat a large, nonstick pan with some oil over medium-high heat. Once hot, add one or two slices (or as many as you can fit) to the pan. Fry over medium-high heat for 3 to 5 minutes, or until golden brown and crisping. Flip over to cook the second side. Transfer the toast to a plate and cover to keep warm. Repeat to make all eight slices.

4. Serve the French toast warm topped with some dairy-free yogurt, banana, and blueberries. Drizzle over the caramel sauce. Drizzle with maple syrup and dust with confectioners' sugar.

5. Keep the French toast without the toppings in the fridge for 2 to 3 days or in the freezer for 1 month. Defrost at room temperature and warm back up in the pan or toaster.

SERVING SUGGESTIONS AND VARIATIONS
- *Keep this French toast gluten-free by using your favorite gluten-free bread.*
- *If you prefer a more traditional caramel, use the one from the No Yeast Sticky Pecan Buns (page 51) or Banoffee Pie Jars (page 149).*

CHOCOLATE CHIP–RASPBERRY WAFFLES

Serves: 2 to 4 | Time: 30 minutes

There's nothing quite like the smell of golden, sweet waffles in the morning and these chocolate chip–raspberry waffles are the best of both worlds: sweet and fruity, yet rich and chocolatey. They are made with easy-to-find whole foods, and you can customize these with other berries and any number of toppings. I love these with lots of whipped coconut cream and more fresh berries.

For the Waffles

- ¼ cup (36 g) ground chia seeds plus 10 tablespoons (148 ml) water
- 1 cup (140 g) all-purpose or gluten-free flour
- 2 teaspoons (9 g) baking powder
- 2 cups (200 g) oat flour
- ¼ cup (35 g) coconut sugar
- A pinch of salt
- 2 cups (480 ml) plant-based milk
- 2 teaspoons (10 ml) lemon juice
- 1 tablespoon (15 ml) vanilla extract
- ½ cup (80 g) dairy-free chocolate chips
- 2 cups (240 g) fresh raspberries
- Oil, for greasing

To Serve

- ½ cup (120 g) whipped dairy-free cream or thick coconut yogurt
- Extra berries
- Maple syrup

1. Stir together the ground chia with water and stir. Leave for 5 minutes to form a gel.
2. Sift the flour and baking powder into a large mixing bowl. Add the oat flour, coconut sugar, and a pinch of salt. Whisk to mix.
3. Pour in the milk, lemon juice, vanilla, and chia gel. Whisk until almost no specks of flour remain, then fold in the chocolate chips and raspberries. Stir until combined and smooth, being careful not to overmix.
4. Allow the batter to rest while the waffle iron heats up. You'll be working in batches; have a covered plate ready or warm the oven.
5. Grease the waffle plates with oil. Add a heaped ¼ cup (about 100 g) of batter per waffle, or enough to fill your waffle iron. Allow the waffles to cook according to your waffle iron instructions. The waffles will be fluffy and golden; allow most of the steam to escape before opening the iron.
6. Keep the waffles warm, and repeat to make all 8 to 10 waffles.
7. To serve: Stack the waffles and serve topped with whipped dairy-free cream, fresh fruit, and maple syrup. Store leftover waffles in a sealed container in the fridge for 2 to 3 days or in the freezer for 1 month.

SERVING SUGGESTIONS AND VARIATIONS

- *Try these waffles with any berries, such as blueberries or strawberries, or you can skip the berries to make chocolate chip waffles.*
- *You can also make these into pancakes using a greased nonstick pan and using about ¼ cup of batter per pancake. Cook until golden.*

3

LUNCH

Whether you are working from home, feeding friends, or looking for your new favorite lunch recipe, this chapter is full of plant-based inspiration. You no longer need to struggle with what to pack in your lunch box or become tired of eating the same boring salad day in and day out.

The recipes in this section of the book are fantastic choices for taking to the office or to a picnic, and they are equally as delicious eaten from your home office or for lazy weekend lunches with family. You'll find veganized versions of lunch staples such as a Mixed Vegetable Frittata (page 77) and hearty Crispy Tofu and Red Pepper Dip Sandwiches (page 79). Wow friends with the easy Almond Satay Tofu Summer Rolls (page 71) and whip up a big Moroccan-Style Quinoa Salad (page 65) for flavor-packed lunches to see you through the week. Then, there is my personal highlight: My Favorite Minestrone Soup (page 63). It's one that I cook for my family most weeks, and it always hits the spot.

MY FAVORITE MINESTRONE SOUP

Serves: 4 to 6 | Time: 40 minutes

This is my family's favorite soup, and I am so excited to share it with you. It is warming and comforting, and it's packed with a rich, herby tomato sauce. The beans add a good dose of protein, and you can use any vegan pasta shapes you like. Finish off this hearty bowl with some torn basil, hunks of bread, and vegan parmesan for a taste of Italy from your own kitchen.

For the Soup
- 1 tablespoon (15 ml) olive oil
- 1 red onion, small dice
- 3 cloves garlic, crushed
- 1 carrot, peeled and chopped small
- 1 red bell pepper, chopped small
- 1 zucchini, chopped small
- ½ teaspoon dried basil
- ½ teaspoon dried oregano
- 1 can mixed beans (drained: 8½ ounces, or 240 g)
- 1 can (14 ounces, or 400 g) chopped tomatoes
- 1 cup (100 g) small pasta shapes
- 2 cups (480 ml) vegetable broth or stock
- 2 tablespoons (32 g) tomato paste (purée)
- Salt and pepper, to taste
- ½ cup loosely chopped fresh basil (a large bunch)

To Serve
- Toasted or fresh bread
- Torn basil
- Homemade Vegan Parmesan (page 167)

1. Add the olive oil to a large saucepan or a deep frying pan over high heat. Add the onion and garlic. Fry off for 5 minutes, until softening. Add the carrot, bell pepper, and zucchini. Fry for 5 minutes to soften the vegetables.
2. Add the dried basil and oregano to the pan. Cook for 1 minute to release the aromas.
3. Add the beans, tomatoes, pasta, broth, tomato paste, salt, and pepper. Stir well and allow the soup to just come to the boil.
4. Place a lid on the pan and lower the heat to simmer for 25 minutes, or until the pasta is soft. Stir occasionally; add more broth as needed.
5. Stir in the basil and cook for 5 minutes to allow the basil to infuse the soup.
6. Serve the minestrone warm with hunks of bread, some extra basil, and my cashew parmesan cheese.
7. Leftover soup will keep in a sealed container in the fridge for 2 to 3 days or in the freezer up to 1 month. Allow the soup to defrost and warm back up with a splash of water.

SERVING SUGGESTIONS AND VARIATIONS
Use any shape pasta for this soup, I like cavatappi, orecchiette, conchigliette, but stars, hearts, or macaroni will work perfectly. You can even break up strands of spaghetti, too.

MOROCCAN-STYLE QUINOA SALAD

Serves: 3 large or 4 smaller plates | Time: 40 minutes plus cooling

When I dream of Moroccan food, I picture sweet but warming aromas, fresh herbs, sticky dried fruits, and tons of color. This salad ticks all of those boxes. Roasting the vegetables with the spices enhances the flavors, while the fresh herbs, chopped nuts, and fruits add texture and life to this make-ahead salad. It is a great choice for lunch boxes or for serving to guests alongside a Falafel Feast (page 69).

For the Quinoa

- ½ cup (90 g) dry quinoa
- 1 cup (240 ml) vegetable broth or stock
- 1 large red onion, sliced
- 1 bell pepper, sliced into strips
- 2 tablespoons (30 ml) olive oil, divided
- 1 teaspoon ground cumin
- ½ teaspoon ground cinnamon
- ¼ teaspoon ground turmeric
- Salt and pepper, to taste
- 1 bulb of garlic
- 1 can chickpeas (drained: 8 ounces, or 240 g)
- 1 small carrot, peeled and grated
- ½ cup (50 g) chopped almonds
- ½ cup (80 g) pomegranate
- 5 large Medjool dates (pitted and chopped: ½ cup, or 100 g)
- 2 tablespoons (8 g) chopped fresh parsley
- 2 tablespoons (12 g) chopped fresh mint

For the Dressing

- 1 tablespoon (15 ml) olive oil
- 1 tablespoon (15 ml) lemon juice
- Zest of ½ lemon
- 1 teaspoon maple syrup
- 1 teaspoon apple cider vinegar
- Salt and pepper, to taste

1. Cook the quinoa according to package instructions using vegetable broth or stock in place of water to add more flavor. Cool for 20 minutes and fluff up with a fork.
2. Preheat the oven to 350°F (180°C, or gas mark 4). Line a large baking tray with parchment paper. Add the red onion and bell pepper and toss with 1 tablespoon (15 ml) of olive oil, cumin, cinnamon, turmeric, salt, and pepper. Roast for 30 minutes, until tender and charring at the edges, tossing halfway through.
3. Trim the top off the garlic bulb to expose the raw garlic and peel away any flaky skin. Rub with 1 tablespoon (15 ml) of olive oil and wrap with tinfoil. Roast for 30 minutes, or until the garlic is soft inside. The garlic will keep in the fridge for 1 week.
4. To make the dressing: In a small bowl, stir together all the ingredients, and season with salt and pepper. Squeeze three of the roasted garlic cloves from the bulb and mash with a fork. Stir into the dressing.
5. Add the quinoa and vegetables to a large mixing bowl with the chickpeas, carrot, almonds, pomegranate, dates, parsley, and mint. Pour over the dressing and toss well.
6. Serve right away or keep leftovers in a sealed container in the fridge for 2 to 3 days.

SERVING SUGGESTIONS AND VARIATIONS

- *Use any grain for this salad; see my How to Build a Nourish Bowl (page 94) for ideas.*
- *You can use other beans and legumes instead of chickpeas, such as cooked lentils, cannellini beans, or butter beans.*

CHICKPEA TABBOULEH WITH LEMON TAHINI

Serves: 4 as a side | Time: 20 minutes

Tabbouleh salads are packed with color, flavor, and texture and that is exactly why I love them. Lots of fresh herbs, a hearty grain, protein-rich chickpeas, and fresh vegetables make this salad a delicious make-ahead lunch for busy days or enjoying as part of a Falafel Feast (page 69). It keeps well so you can make up a big batch at the weekends for tasty lunches throughout the week.

For the Tabbouleh
- ½ cup (90 g) dry quinoa or bulgur wheat
- 1 can chickpeas (drained: 8½ ounces, or 240 g)
- ½ cup (80 g) pomegranate
- 1¼ cups (200 g) cherry tomatoes, chopped small
- 1½ cups (200 g) cucumber, chopped small
- 2 tablespoons (2 g) chopped fresh cilantro
- 2 tablespoons (12 g) chopped fresh mint
- 2 tablespoons (30 ml) olive oil
- 1 tablespoon (15 ml) lemon juice
- 1 tablespoon (15 ml) apple cider vinegar
- 1 tablespoon (15 ml) maple syrup
- 1 teaspoon Dijon mustard
- Salt and pepper, to taste

For the Lemon Tahini
- 2 tablespoons (15 g) runny tahini
- 1½ tablespoons (25 ml) lemon juice
- ½ teaspoon maple syrup
- ½ teaspoon garlic granules or 1 small clove garlic, crushed
- Salt and pepper, to taste

1. Cook the quinoa according to package instructions and allow to cool.
2. Add the chickpeas, pomegranate, tomatoes, and cucumber to a large mixing bowl. Stir well.
3. Add the cooled cooked quinoa, cilantro, and mint. Toss to combine.
4. In a small bowl, stir together the olive oil, lemon juice, apple cider vinegar, maple syrup, Dijon mustard, salt, and pepper. Pour over the tabbouleh salad.
5. To make the lemon tahini: In a small bowl, stir together all the ingredients with 1 to 2 tablespoons (15 to 28 ml) of water to reach a pourable, smooth sauce.
6. Serve the chickpea tabbouleh drizzled with the lemon tahini in bowls.
7. Leftovers will keep in a sealed container in the fridge for 2 to 3 days.

SERVING SUGGESTIONS AND VARIATIONS
- *Use any grain for this salad; see my How to Build a Nourish Bowl (page 94) for a list of other grains.*
- *Other beans and legumes, such as cooked lentils, cannellini beans, or butter beans, will work in place of the chickpeas.*

FALAFEL FEAST

Serves: 4 to 6 | Time: 40 minutes

I called this falafel recipe a feast because it's best served with lots of dips, spreads, and sides. It is perfect to enjoy with friends and family. It relies on simple whole-food ingredients, a few cupboard staples, and fresh herbs. Plus, I love that the falafel are baked but turn out just as crispy as fried!

For the Roasted Vegetables
- 2 bell peppers, sliced into strips
- 2 large red onions, sliced into strips
- 2 tablespoons (30 ml) olive oil
- 1 teaspoon ground cumin
- ½ teaspoon hot smoked paprika
- ½ teaspoon garlic granules

For the Falafel
- 2 cans chickpeas (drained: 16 ounces, or 480 g)
- 6 cloves roasted garlic, or 3 cloves peeled fresh garlic
- 1 teaspoon ground cumin
- 1 teaspoon hot smoked paprika
- Zest of 1 lemon
- 1 tablespoon (15 ml) olive oil, plus extra for baking
- 1 tablespoon (6 g) chickpea/gram flour
- ½ cup (30 g) fresh parsley, loosely packed (stalks too)
- ½ teaspoon baking soda
- Salt and pepper, to taste

For the Hummus
- 2 cans chickpeas (drained: 16 ounces, or 480 g; save the aquafaba)
- 4 cloves roasted garlic or 2 cloves fresh garlic
- 2 teaspoons (5 g) ground cumin
- ½ cup (120 g) runny tahini
- 2 tablespoons (30 ml) olive oil
- ½–1 cup (120–240 ml) aquafaba

To Serve
- Chickpea Tabbouleh with Lemon Tahini (page 67)
- Two-Ingredient Flatbreads (page 121)
- Roasted Red Pepper Dip (page 79)

1. Preheat the oven to 350°F (180°C, or gas mark 4). Line two to four large baking trays with parchment paper.
2. To make the roasted vegetables: Toss everything together and lay out on a tray, trying not to overlap too much. Roast for 30 minutes, or until tender and charring.
3. Meanwhile, make the falafel: Add everything to a food processor or blender and blend to a chunky mix that holds together when pressed between your two fingers. Divide the mixture into twenty small pieces and roll into balls.
4. Place the falafel balls on the baking trays and brush lightly with olive oil. Bake for 15 minutes, or until crisp and golden.
5. To make the hummus: Add all the ingredients to a food processor or blender, starting with ½ cup (120 ml) of the reserved aquafaba and blend until smooth and creamy. Stop to scrape down the sides; add more aquafaba as needed to reach your preferred consistency.

(CONTINUED ON PAGE 70)

(CONTINUED FROM PAGE 69)

6. Serve the baked falafel alongside the roasted vegetables with the creamy hummus and any extra sides.
7. Store leftovers in separate containers in the fridge for 2 to 3 days.

SERVING SUGGESTIONS AND VARIATIONS

- *For the best tasting hummus, I like to use roasted garlic (see the Moroccan-Style Quinoa Salad, page 65).*
- *For the creamiest hummus, I highly recommend removing the skins off the chickpeas first. Pour the drained chickpeas onto a tea towel and place a second one on top. Rub the chickpeas quite vigorously to encourage the skins off, then pick off the stubborn skins. Throw out the skins and blend the chickpeas as above.*

ALMOND SATAY TOFU
SUMMER ROLLS

Serves: 3 to 4 (makes 12 to 14 rolls) | Time: 30 minutes

Summer rolls always make me smile and think of the sunshine; they are just so vibrant and delicious, and fun to make. These summer rolls are filled with an array of crunchy raw vegetables and a sticky almond satay tofu—with extra sauce for dipping. Add some vermicelli noodles and get rolling!

For the Almond Satay

- ¼ cup (60 g) runny, smooth almond butter
- 2 tablespoons (28 ml) tamari
- 2 tablespoons (30 ml) maple syrup
- 1 tablespoon (15 ml) sesame oil
- 2 small cloves garlic, crushed
- 1-inch (2½-cm) piece garlic, peeled and grated
- 1–2 teaspoons (5–10 ml) hot chile sauce
- 2 tablespoons (28 ml) lime juice
- Salt and pepper, to taste

For the Rolls

- 10½ ounces (300 g) extra-firm tofu
- 1 bell pepper
- 1 large carrot
- 2-inch (5-cm) cucumber
- 4½ ounces (120 g) red cabbage
- 1 tablespoon (15 ml) sesame or olive oil
- 3½ ounces (100 g) vermicelli rice noodles
- 40 fresh mint leaves
- 12–14 rice paper sheets

1. For the almond satay dressing: In a small bowl, stir together all the ingredients until smooth. Season with salt and pepper.
2. Slice the tofu into 2½-inch (5-cm) strips, aiming to have 12 to 14 strips. Similarly, slice the bell pepper, carrot, and cucumber into thin strips of the same length. Shred the red cabbage to roughly match the length of the other vegetables.
3. To make the tofu: Heat the oil in a large, nonstick, frying pan over high heat. Fry off the tofu strips for a few minutes, until golden and crisp, on each side. Work in batches over medium-high heat and continue to fry off all the tofu. Add all the tofu back in the hot pan with 2 tablespoons (28 ml) of the almond satay sauce and stir quickly to evenly coat the tofu. Remove from the pan and allow to cool briefly.
4. Cook the noodles according to package instructions. Drain under cold water to cool them off and prevent the noodles from sticking.
5. Have all the vegetables, noodles, tofu, and mint leaves laid out in front of you.
6. Fill a shallow, wide bowl with warm water and dip in one rice paper sheet at a time. Allow the sheet to soften slightly (check the instructions on your package) and place on a chopping board.
7. Fill the rice paper rolls: Lay on a few mint leaves in the middle and top with noodles, tofu, and a few strips of vegetables. Lift the bottom of the rice paper up and over the filling gently but tightly. Tuck the sides of the rice paper inwards and continue to roll (like a burrito). Place aside and continue to make all the summer rolls.

(CONTINUED ON PAGE 73)

(CONTINUED FROM PAGE 71)

8. Chill in the fridge for 20 minutes, then use a sharp knife to slice each roll in half.
9. Serve the summer rolls alongside the remaining almond satay sauce.
10. Leftovers will keep well in a sealed container in the fridge for 2 to 3 days.

SERVING SUGGESTIONS AND VARIATIONS

- *Swap the almond butter for any other nut or seed butter.*
- *These are great for sharing and grazing, and feel free to change up the vegetables.*

SWEET POTATO, KALE, AND SUN-DRIED TOMATO SALAD

Serves: 4 as a main, or 6 as a side | Time: 60 minutes

This is my favorite kind of meal-worthy salad. It has everything you need: whole grains, lots of colorful vegetables, a creamy dressing, a nice crunch on top and tons of flavor. Even kale haters might come around; the trick is to massage the kale first to take away the bitterness and toughness of the leaves.

For the Sweet Potatoes
- 2 medium sweet potatoes (trimmed: 1.1 lb., or 500 g)
- 2 red onions
- 1 tablespoon (15 ml) olive oil
- ½ teaspoon garlic granules
- ¼ teaspoon chile flakes
- Salt and pepper, to taste

For the Salad
- ½ cup (90 g) buckwheat or other grain
- 4 cups (100 g) shredded kale
- 1 can butter beans (drained: 8½ ounces, or 240 g)
- ¾ cup (120 g) chopped sun-dried tomatoes
- ¼ cup (56 g) crumbled vegan feta cheese
- 2 tablespoons (14 g) chopped almonds or seeds

For the Vinaigrette
- 3 tablespoons (45 ml) extra-virgin olive oil
- 1½ tablespoons (25 ml) balsamic vinegar
- 1½ tablespoons (25 ml) lemon juice
- 2 teaspoons (10 ml) maple syrup or vegan honey
- 1 teaspoon Dijon mustard
- Salt and pepper, to taste

1. Preheat the oven to 350°F (180°C, or gas mark 4). Line a large baking tray with parchment paper. Chop the sweet potatoes into 1-inch (2½-cm) chunks and slice the red onions into thick slices. Add to a large bowl and toss with the olive oil, garlic granules, chile flakes, salt, and pepper. Transfer to the baking tray and roast for 40 to 45 minutes, until tender and crisp. Stir the tray well halfway through. Allow to cool slightly.
2. Cook the buckwheat according to package instructions. Allow to cool briefly while you prepare the rest of the salad.
3. Add all the vinaigrette ingredients with some salt and pepper to a glass jar with a lid. Seal the lid and shake the jar to mix the ingredients together.
4. Add the kale to the same large bowl (no need to rinse it out). Add 1 tablespoon (15 ml) of the vinaigrette. Massage the kale with your hands for 1 minute to wilt the leaves; they will turn vibrant green.
5. To the kale, add the cooked buckwheat, butter beans, most of the sun-dried tomatoes, and the roasted sweet potatoes and red onions. Pour over most of the dressing and toss well.
6. Serve in a large bowl or four smaller bowls topped with the remaining sun-dried tomatoes. Sprinkle over the feta cheese, almonds, and the extra dressing.
7. Eat right away, or cover well and keep in a sealed container in the fridge for 2 to 3 days.

SERVING SUGGESTIONS AND VARIATIONS
If you don't like butter beans, swap these for other beans, such as cannellini or navy beans, or try chickpeas, too.

MIXED VEGETABLE FRITTATA WITH ROASTED NEW POTATOES

Serves: 2 as a main, 4 as a lunch | Time: 60 minutes

I have to admit, I have never craved "eggy" food since becoming vegan, but I had been on a mission to create the best egg-free and dairy-free frittata and I think I have cracked it. This frittata is loaded with vegetables and is "eggy" from the tofu, chickpea flour, and the magic addition of kala namak (black salt). Serve slices of this frittata with roasted new potatoes and red onions for a delicious light lunch or dinner.

For the Vegetables
- 4 ounces (110 g) mushrooms
- 1 small sweet potato (4 oz, or 110 g)
- ½ bell pepper
- ½ zucchini
- 1 teaspoon olive oil
- 2 cloves garlic, crushed
- 1 cup (30 g) baby spinach
- 1 scallion, chopped
- Salt and pepper, to taste

For the "Eggy" Mix
- 7 ounces (200 g) extra-firm tofu
- ½ cup (50 g) chickpea/gram flour
- ½ cup (120 ml) unsweetened plant-based milk
- 2 tablespoons (10 g) nutritional yeast
- ½ teaspoon garlic granules
- ½ teaspoon kala namak (black salt; optional)
- ¼ teaspoon hot smoked paprika
- ¼ teaspoon ground turmeric
- Salt and pepper, to taste

For the Potatoes
- 1¼ lb. (500 g) new potatoes
- 2 red onions
- 1–2 tablespoons (15–30 ml) olive oil
- ¼ teaspoon chile flakes
- Salt and pepper, to taste

To Serve (optional)
- Fresh arugula
- Vegan feta cheese, crumbled
- Sliced tomatoes

1. Preheat the oven to 350°F (180°C, or gas mark 4). Lightly grease an 8-inch (20-cm) pan or dish. Line a large baking tray with parchment paper.
2. To make the vegetables: Slice the mushrooms. Scrub and chop the sweet potato into chunks. Chop the pepper and zucchini in similar-sized chunks, too. Heat the olive oil in a large frying pan. Add the mushrooms, garlic, salt, and pepper. Fry for 5 minutes, until softened. Add the sweet potatoes, and fry for 2 to 3 minutes. Add the bell pepper and zucchini; this way we do not overwhelm the pan! Stir through the spinach to wilt the leaves. Remove the pan from the heat, cover it, and set it aside.
3. To make the "eggy" mix: Add everything to a blender and process until really smooth. Season with salt and pepper.
4. Add the egg mixture to a large mixing bowl with most of the vegetables (save some vegetables for the top) and stir well. Pour into the greased dish, smooth over the top and arrange the reserved vegetables and scallion on top.

(CONTINUED ON PAGE 78)

(CONTINUED FROM PAGE 77)

5. Cover with foil and bake for 25 minutes. Uncover and bake for 10 to 15 minutes, until golden and browning at the edges and firm all the way through.

6. While the frittata cooks, make the potatoes: Slice any large potatoes into halves or quarters to make 1-inch (2½-cm) cubes. Chop the red onions. Add both to the tray with the olive oil, chile flakes, salt, and pepper. Toss well and bake at the same time as the frittata for 45 minutes, or until crisp and golden, tossing halfway through.

7. Allow the frittata to cool for 10 minutes in the dish before slicing and serving with the roasted potatoes. Sprinkle over some fresh arugula, vegan feta cheese, and tomatoes (if using).

SERVING SUGGESTIONS AND VARIATIONS

- *Use any vegetables for this frittata; try swapping in chopped broccoli, cubed squash, eggplant (aubergine), or kale.*
- *Kala namak is also known as black salt. It adds a strong "eggy" flavor and smell to savory dishes. It is delicious here, but not essential.*

CRISPY TOFU AND ROASTED RED PEPPER DIP SANDWICHES

Makes: 2 large or 4 regular sandwiches | Time: 40 minutes

Gone are the days of boring plant-based sandwiches. These are packed with flavor and color thanks to roasted red pepper dip. It is similar to a muhammara dip, a spicy dip made from roasted red peppers that usually uses breadcrumbs and is found in a lot of Turkish and Syrian cuisine. It is delicious: you can dip, spread, and swirl this into many meals.

For the Roasted Red Pepper Dip
- 2 sweet or bell peppers, whole
- 1 teaspoon olive oil
- ⅓ heaped cup (40 g) walnuts
- ¼ cup (25 g) oats
- 1 tablespoon (20 g) pomegranate molasses
- 1 tablespoon (15 ml) lemon juice
- ½ teaspoon ground cumin
- ½ teaspoon chile flakes
- ½ teaspoon smoked paprika
- ½ teaspoon garlic granules or 1 clove garlic
- Salt and pepper, to taste

For the Sandwiches
- 7 ounces (200 g) extra-firm tofu
- 1 tablespoon (15 ml) olive oil
- 1 teaspoon nutritional yeast (optional)
- ¼ teaspoon chile flakes
- 4 large or 8 regular slices of sourdough bread
- 2–4 tablespoons (28–56 g) Hummus (page 69)
- ⅔ cup (100 g) cherry tomatoes, sliced
- 2 handfuls salad leaves

1. To make the roasted red pepper dip: Preheat the oven to 400°F (200°C, or gas mark 6). Line a tray with parchment paper. Add the peppers to the tray and lightly brush with oil. Roast for 15 minutes, turn over and roast for 15 minutes, until the skin starts to char. Carefully transfer the peppers to a small bowl and cover for 10 minutes, or until cool enough to handle. Peel the skins off the peppers and discard the seeds inside, place the peppers to one side.

2. Add the walnuts and oats to a food processor and blitz to a fine meal. Add the roasted peppers and all the other ingredients and blend to reach a smooth mix that's slightly chunky. Season with salt and pepper. Pour into a small bowl, where the dip will continue to thicken. Set aside.

3. To make the tofu: Slice the block in half and slice each half into four thin strips so you have eight in total. Sprinkle the nutritional yeast (if using) and chile flakes over both sides of the tofu. Heat a large, nonstick pan with some of the olive oil over high heat. Once hot, add the tofu and fry for 2 to 3 minutes, or until golden and crisp. Flip over and fry the second side until golden. Repeat to cook all eight pieces of tofu, adding oil to the pan as needed. Once cool, the tofu will keep in the fridge for 2 to 3 days in a sealed container.

(CONTINUED ON PAGE 81)

(CONTINUED FROM PAGE 79)

4. To assemble the sandwiches: Spread half the slices with the roasted red pepper dip. (You will have dip leftover extra can be stored in a sealed container in the fridge for 5 to 7 days.) Top with some salad leaves, a piece of tofu, tomatoes, and a second slice of tofu. Spread the other slices of bread with hummus and top the tofu sandwiches. Slice in half and enjoy.

SERVING SUGGESTIONS AND VARIATIONS

- *To keep these sandwiches gluten-free, use gluten-free certified oats in the dip and make sure your bread does not contain gluten.*
- *Pomegranate molasses boasts so much flavor and is typical for red pepper dips, but you can use maple syrup instead.*

TAHINI, AVOCADO, AND TOMATO PASTA SALAD WITH CRUNCHY CHICKPEAS

Serves: 4 | Time: 40 minutes

Pasta salads are a staple for picnics, lunch boxes, and easy summery meals. This tahini, avocado, and tomato pasta salad takes things up a notch with crunchy roasted chickpeas and a creamy, lemony tahini dressing. Serve this salad on its own for a well-rounded and vibrant lunch or dinner, or have it alongside a few other salads, too.

For the Chickpeas
- 1 can chickpeas (drained: 8½ ounces, or 240 g)
- 1 teaspoon olive oil
- Salt and pepper, to taste

For the Pasta Salad
- 10½ ounces (300 g) small pasta shapes
- 2 cups (300 g) cherry tomatoes, halved or quartered
- ¼ cup (12 g) chopped fresh basil
- 2 avocados, peeled and chopped
- 2–4 tablespoons (12–24 g) Homemade Vegan Parmesan (page 167)

For the Tahini Dressing
- 3 tablespoons (45 g) runny tahini
- 2 tablespoons (28 ml) lemon juice
- Zest of ½ lemon
- 1 tablespoon (15 ml) olive oil
- 2–3 tablespoons (28–45 ml) reserved pasta water
- Salt and pepper, to taste

1. To make the chickpeas: Preheat the oven to 350°F (180°C, or gas mark 4). Line a large tray with parchment paper. Pat the chickpeas dry and add to the tray with the olive oil, salt, and pepper. Toss well. Roast for 30 minutes, or until golden and crispy; stir well halfway through.
2. Cook the pasta according to package instructions until al dente; reserve some of the cooking water. Allow the pasta to cool down, then use your hands to break apart any pasta that has stuck together.
3. To make the tahini dressing: In a small bowl, add all the ingredients and season with salt and pepper. Stir together until smooth and pourable.
4. Add the pasta to a large mixing bowl. Add most of the tomatoes, most of the basil, and most of the avocado, reserving some to garnish. Stir in half the chickpeas and all the dressing. Stir well.
5. Serve the pasta salad in bowls topped with the remaining tomatoes, basil, avocado, and chickpeas with a sprinkling of vegan parmesan.
6. Leftovers will keep in a sealed container in the fridge for 2 to 3 days. The avocado will brown over time; to freshen the pasta back up, add 1 to 2 teaspoons (5 to 10 ml) of lemon juice and stir well.

SERVING SUGGESTIONS AND VARIATIONS
You can add lots of other vegetables, such as sweet corn and cooked peas, into this pasta salad. Try swapping the chickpeas for baked tofu or fresh cannellini beans.

4

DINNER

In this next chapter, you'll find some of my favorite main meals to make: from quick, midweek stir-fries to comforting bowls of chili to enjoy with the family. These are great for meal planning and prepping, or enjoy them as a plant-based dinner to change up your regular rota. There's something here for everyone. Plus, I give you a step-by-step guide of how I design my Nourish Bowls (page 94), so you'll never lack inspiration again.

All the recipes are designed with you in mind, so whether you are cooking for one, two, or a crowd, the recipes are easily adapted to suit your needs. I am so excited to share with you my Homemade Sweet Potato Gnocchi (page 87), my vibrant Mexican-Style Loaded Sweet Potato Wedges (page 89), and so many others . . . Buon appetito!

HOMEMADE SWEET POTATO GNOCCHI WITH TOMATOES AND KALE

Serves: 4 | Time: 20 minutes prep plus 20 minutes cooking

If you haven't made homemade gnocchi before, you are in for a treat. Unlike some pasta recipes, which can be involved, this dough has just three basic ingredients and comes together easily. Even though it's gluten-free, the texture is perfect: it's pillowy soft in the middle and slightly crisp and charred at the edges after a quick pan-fry in vegan butter. It is so satisfying to sit down to a bowl of homemade pasta.

For the Sweet Potato Gnocchi
- 2 cups (500 g) mashed sweet potato (see note on page 88 to make your own)
- 1 cup (140 g) all-purpose or gluten-free flour, plus extra for dusting
- 2 tablespoons (10 g) nutritional yeast (optional)
- Salt and pepper, to taste

For the Vegetables
- 2⅔ cups (400 g) cherry tomatoes
- 2 cups (182 g) broccoli florets
- 1 teaspoon olive oil
- 2 tablespoons (28 g) vegan butter
- 8 leaves lacinato kale, de-stemmed and torn (4 packed cups)
- 2 tablespoons (18 g) pine nuts

To Serve
- Fresh arugula or other greens
- Homemade Vegan Parmesan (page 167)
- Chile flakes

1. To make the gnocchi: Add the sweet potato, flour, nutritional yeast (if using), salt, and pepper to a large mixing bowl. Stir well. Bring to a rough dough and transfer to a floured work surface.
2. Use your hands to knead to a ball of dough. Divide into eight equal pieces; it helps to weigh them. Roll each piece into a 7-inch (18-cm)-long log. Repeat to make eight equal logs, then slice each log into seven pieces.
3. Gently roll a piece of gnocchi into the tines of a fork (or use a gnocchi board) to make grooves. This helps the sauce to stick. Repeat with all the gnocchi.
4. Preheat the oven to 350°F (180°C, or gas mark 4). Add the tomatoes and broccoli to a baking tray. Drizzle with the olive oil, and season with salt and pepper. Roast for 20 minutes, or until the tomatoes have burst and the broccoli is crisp.
5. To cook the gnocchi: Bring a large pan of salted water to a boil. Once bubbling, drop in eight to ten pieces of gnocchi; do not overcrowd the pan. Cook for 2 to 3 minutes. Once cooked, the gnocchi will feel spongy but firm between your fingers and they will naturally float to the top of the water.
6. Remove the cooked gnocchi with a slotted spoon. Transfer them to a large bowl. Repeat to make all the gnocchi.
7. Once the gnocchi are boiled, heat the vegan butter in a large frying pan over medium-high heat. Add the kale, pine nuts, and gnocchi. Fry for 5 to 8 minutes, or until the greens are crisping and the gnocchi are golden in color; it is best to do this in two batches.
8. Stir the cooked tomatoes and broccoli, and divide them among four bowls. Top with the fresh arugula, vegan parmesan, and chile flakes. Store any leftovers in a sealed container in the fridge for 2 to 3 days.

(CONTINUED ON PAGE 88)

(CONTINUED FROM PAGE 87)

NOTES

- *To make your own mashed sweet potato: Prepare two large sweet potatoes by puncturing them all over with a knife. Place them on a tray in the middle of an oven preheated to 400°F (200°C, or gas mark 6). Bake for 50 to 60 minutes, or until tender inside. Allow to cool slightly, then peel away the skin; you can eat the skin or save for another recipe, if you like! Add the sweet potato flesh to a small bowl and mash very well with a fork; or add it to a blender and blend until smooth. Make sure the sweet potato is cool before making the gnocchi.*
- *You can make the gnocchi ahead of time for this recipe. Once it has been made and shaped but not boiled, store the gnocchi in a sealed container in the fridge for 2 to 3 days or freeze the gnocchi for up to 1 month. Alternately, refrigerate or freeze the boiled gnocchi.*

MEXICAN-STYLE LOADED SWEET POTATO WEDGES

Serves: 4 to 6 | Time: 10 minutes prep plus 35 minutes cooking

This, to me, is pure joy as a finger-food. These wedges look beautifully abundant, and they taste amazing. Packed with delicious vegetables and garlicky tomato black beans, and topped off with fresh coconut yogurt dressing, there's a lot of flavor in every bite.

For the Sweet Potato Wedges
- 2 large or 3 medium sweet potatoes (22 ounces, or 650 g)
- 1½ tablespoons (25 ml) olive oil
- 1 teaspoon ground cumin
- Salt and pepper, to taste

For the Avocado-Tomato Salsa
- 1⅓ cup (200 g) cherry tomatoes
- 1 avocado
- 2 tablespoons (2 g) chopped fresh cilantro
- 2 tablespoons (28 ml) lime juice
- Salt and pepper, to taste

For the Black Beans
- 1 teaspoon olive oil
- 2 cloves garlic
- 1 can black beans (drained: 8 ounces, or 240 g)
- ½ teaspoon ground cumin
- ½ teaspoon hot smoked paprika
- Salt and pepper, to taste
- 2 tablespoons (32 g) tomato paste (purée)
- 1 tablespoon (15 ml) water

To Serve
- ¼ cup (60 g) coconut yogurt
- 2 tablespoons (28 ml) lime juice
- Fresh sweetcorn
- Chopped scallion
- Lime wedges
- Chopped fresh cilantro
- Seeds or Dukkah (page 97)
- Chile flakes

1. Preheat the oven to 400°F (200°C, or gas mark 6). Line a baking tray with parchment paper.
2. Scrub the sweet potatoes and slice off the ends. Chop into wedges and add to the tray. Drizzle the potatoes with olive oil, then toss with the cumin, salt, and pepper. Bake for 35 minutes, or until tender and crisping at the edges. Toss the potatoes halfway through the cooking time.
3. To make the avocado-tomato salsa: Chop the tomatoes small, and peel, de-stone, and cube the avocado. Add the cilantro and lime juice to a small mixing bowl. Season with salt and pepper. Toss well and set side.
4. To make the black beans: Add the olive oil to a small saucepan or frying pan over medium heat and heat through. Add the garlic and fry for 1 to 2 minutes, until fragrant. Add the black beans, cumin, hot smoked paprika, salt, and pepper. Mix well for 1 minute before adding the tomato paste and water. Continue to mix well over medium heat for 5 minutes, gently mashing the beans with the spoon. Add a splash of water if it starts to stick.

(CONTINUED ON PAGE 91)

(CONTINUED FROM PAGE 89)

5. To make the dressing: Stir together the yogurt and lime juice.
6. Serve on a large platter as shown here or use four or six individual plates. Start with the sweet potato wedges, then top with the black beans followed by the salsa, yogurt, and your chosen garnishes.
7. This is best eaten right away or store leftovers in individual containers (otherwise the wedges will soften too much) for 2 to 3 days.

SERVING SUGGESTIONS AND VARIATIONS

- *These wedges are also great to make as side dishes to any of the Nourish Bowls (page 95) or lunch or dinner recipes in this book—or make them as a savory snack on their own.*
- *Leftover black beans and salsa are delicious with crackers or on bread, too.*

SMOKY SWEET POTATO–MIXED BEAN CHILI

Serves: 4 | Time: 10 minutes prep plus 35 minutes cooking

This "chili non-carne" is a family favorite—and for a good reason! It's warming, wholesome, and hearty. Full of fiber and protein from sweet potatoes and beans, this one-pot meal is a winter staple at my house. I hope you'll love it, too. It's even got a secret added ingredient to make it really rich and delicious.

For the Chili
- 1 tablespoon (15 ml) olive oil
- 1 onion, small dice
- 4 cloves garlic, crushed
- 1 large sweet potato, peeled and cubed (3 cups, or 400 g)
- 1 red bell pepper, cubed (1 cup, or 150 g)
- ½ teaspoon chile flakes
- 1½ teaspoons ground cumin
- 1 teaspoon hot smoked paprika
- 1 teaspoon dried oregano
- 1 can mixed beans (drained: 8½ ounces, or 240 g)
- 1 can chopped tomatoes (14 ounces, or 400 g)
- 2 tablespoons (32 g) tomato paste (purée)
- 1 cup (240 ml) vegetable stock or water
- 1 tablespoon (5 g) cacao or cocoa powder
- Salt and pepper, to taste

To Serve
- 2 cups (350 g) cooked rice
- Avocado
- Vegan sour cream or yogurt
- Tortilla chips
- Vegan cheese
- Fresh cilantro

1. Heat the olive oil in a large, nonstick pan over medium-high heat. Once hot, add the onion and garlic. Cook over high heat for 3 to 5 minutes, or until turning translucent.
2. Add the sweet potato and bell pepper. Fry for 5 minutes to soften the vegetables.
3. Add in the chile flakes, cumin, hot smoked paprika, and oregano. Fry for 1 minute, stirring well, until fragrant.
4. Pour in the beans, tomatoes, tomato paste, vegetable stock, and cacao powder. Season with salt and pepper. Stir well, bring to the boil, and cook with a lid on over medium heat for 25 to 30 minutes, until the potatoes are soft.
5. Serve the chili with cooked rice, avocado, vegan sour cream, tortilla chips, vegan cheese, and cilantro.
6. Once cool, the chili will store in a sealed container in the fridge for 2 to 3 days or in the freezer for up to 1 month.

SERVING SUGGESTIONS AND VARIATIONS
- *Use any beans for this chili. I love to use canned mixed beans for variety, but kidney, pinto, black, or cannellini beans would also be great.*
- *Make sure to cook up a big batch to freeze for later, as it tastes even better after the flavors meld.*

HOW TO BUILD A NOURISH BOWL

Nourish bowls are my favorite meals to make for myself and my friends as you can have a little bit of everything in one bowl. Also known as Buddha Bowls, they pack so much into one meal: delicious veggies, a rainbow of color, and a variety of textures. It is hard not to love them! While these bowls can be quite informal, there are some fundamentals and tricks that I have picked up along the way that I am sharing here for what I consider the perfect nourish bowl.

Choose Your Grain

This is the base for your bowl and who doesn't love a foundation of whole-grain goodness? There are so many to choose from, and it's good to come back to this list when you tire of eating the same rice or quinoa every day! A lot of the grains are naturally gluten-free, too.

- Rice: including white, brown, red, black, or sticky rice
- Quinoa: white or tricolor; it is actually a pseudo-cereal
- Buckwheat: contains no wheat despite the name
- Couscous: usually contains wheat
- Bulgar wheat: does contain wheat
- Amaranth: a very small pseudo-cereal
- Barley or pearl barley
- Oats: more versatile than just for breakfast
- Millet: small, round seed-grain

Pick Your Protein

Following a vegan and vegetarian diet, it is very easy to meet all your protein needs as long as you know where to find it. Here are a few great sources for the best nourish bowls.

- Tofu: extra-firm is best for frying and baking
- Tempeh: made from fermented soybeans is also great for baking or frying
- Seitan: made from wheat gluten
- Chickpeas: great for hummus, falafel, and baking
- Beans: edamame, butter, black, red, kidney, pinto, cannellini . . .
- Lentils: red split, green, black, brown, puy, beluga . . .

Flavor Time!

When it comes to making nourish bowls tasty, it's important to pick a few flavors, spices, or blends to really make the protein and the vegetables taste great. Here are a few of my favorite spices and herbs to add:

- Ground cumin: for Indian, Moroccan, or Mexican-style foods
- Hot smoked paprika or regular smoked paprika: for Spanish and Mexican foods
- Turmeric: for curries and other vibrant meals
- Garlic: roasted, or crushed and fried
- Ginger: fresh is best for adding to savory meals
- Chile: flakes or fresh
- Harissa: a delicious chile pepper paste (Try rose harissa.)
- Chipotle: smoked and dried chipotle/jalapeño paste
- Pesto: great for Mediterranean flavors
- Dried basil, oregano, and mixed herbs: also good for Mediterranean flavors
- Dried or fresh thyme, rosemary, and sage: delicious for roast dinners

(CONTINUED ON PAGE 96)

(CONTINUED FROM PAGE 94)

Cooked Vegetables

For my nourish bowls, I like to play around with vegetables: both cooked and un-cooked. When it comes to cooking them, there are so many ways to prepare them depending on the flavor pairings. You can roast, steam, stir-fry, grill, or griddle . . . you name it. Here are some of my favorite cooked vegetables to add to bowls.

- Broccoli
- Eggplant
- Zucchini
- Tomatoes
- Sweet Potato
- Squash or pumpkin
- Bell pepper
- Cauliflower
- Mushrooms
- Carrot
- Parsnips
- Kale and other sturdy greens
- Peas (frozen or fresh)

Raw Vegetables and Fruits

Along with cooked vegetables, fresh or raw vegetables (and fruits, too) are delicious in nourish bowls. They can add great crunch and coolness. Here are a few to choose from.

- Cucumber
- Tomatoes
- Bell pepper
- Carrot, especially grated
- Cabbage: red, white, Chinese leaf
- Salad leaves, such as spinach, arugula, watercress, or lettuce, are great as a base
- Scallions
- Fresh herbs
- Blueberries, strawberries, and raspberries (when in season)
- Apple: sliced apple in particular
- Cherries
- Pomegranate
- Stoned fruits, such as peaches, plums, nectarines, are great sliced

Get Saucy with a Dressing

Perhaps one of the most important components is the dressing, as it brings together all the separate components in a nourish bowl. There are so many different ones to choose from depending on the flavors in your bowl.

- Balsamic vinaigrette
- Zesty vinaigrette (page 165 [Kale, Pomegranate, and Almond Winter Salad])
- Tahini dressing (page 97 [Harissa Mediterranean Vegetables with Crunchy Chickpeas])
- Olive oil, lemon, and salt
- Hummus dressing (thin down your hummus with some lemon juice for a quick dressing)
- Lime-y coconut yogurt (page 107 [Mexican Jackfruit Stuffed Sweet Potatoes])
- Almond Satay (page 71 [Fresh Summer Rolls with Almond Satay Tofu])

Time for Crunch

One of the easiest ways to take a bowl to the next level is to add crunch. It seems simple, but an added layer of texture can make a nourish bowl more exciting and inviting. You only need 1 or 2 tablespoons (weight varies) of these to elevate your bowl.

- Dukkah (page 97 [Harissa Mediterranean Vegetables with Crunchy Chickpeas])
- Chopped nuts and seeds: for added flavor, dry-fry them for 5 minutes, until fragrant
- Sesame seeds: especially good with Asian cuisines
- Roasted beans, legumes, and chickpeas (store-bought or page 97 [Crunchy Chickpeas])
- Crushed tortilla chips
- Broken up crackers (page 119 [Homemade Seedy Crackers])

Something Creamy to Finish

This is an optional extra, but some bowls benefit from yet another dimension on top of the dressing and the crunch. These ingredients also add some fat, which may benefit some bowls more than others. Creamy extras can be smaller in quantity, but they add a mighty punch.

- Avocado
- Vegan cheese, such as crumbled feta cheese or grated dairy-free cheese
- Cream cheese (page 135 [Garlic Herb Cashew Cheese])

HARISSA-ROASTED VEGETABLE WITH CRUNCHY CHICKPEAS AND DUKKAH

Serves: 4 | Time: 5 minutes prep plus 30 minutes cooking

This is one of my go-to nourish bowls filled with foods that could never bore me. It has a simple whole-grain for the base, tender chunks of harissa-roasted vegetables, and protein-rich crunchy chickpeas. It's served with the creamiest, tastiest tahini dressing along with a good sprinkle of dukkah.

For the Harissa Vegetables and Chickpeas
- 1 medium eggplant
- 1 medium zucchini
- 1 red bell pepper
- 2 tablespoons (30 g) harissa paste
- 1 tablespoon (15 ml) olive oil
- Salt and pepper, to taste
- 1 can chickpeas (drained: 8½ ounces, or 240 g)

For the Dukkah
- ⅓ cup (50 g) hazelnuts, skin-off
- 1 teaspoon black sesame seeds
- 1 teaspoon white sesame seeds
- 1 teaspoon cumin seeds
- 1 teaspoon fennel seeds
- Salt and pepper, to taste

For the Tahini Dressing
- ¼ cup (60 g) runny tahini
- 1 tablespoon (15 ml) lemon juice
- 1 tablespoon (15 ml) tamari or soy sauce
- 1 teaspoon maple syrup
- 2–4 tablespoons (28–60 ml) water
- Salt and pepper, to taste

To Serve
- 2 cups (370 g) cooked quinoa
- Fresh cilantro or parsley
- Pomegranate

1. Preheat the oven to 350°F (180°C, or gas mark 4). Line three baking trays with parchment paper.
2. To make the vegetables: Chop the eggplant, zucchini, and bell pepper into thin strips or small chunks. Add them to a large mixing bowl. Add the harissa paste and olive oil, and season with salt and pepper. Toss well. Pour onto one baking sheet, leaving the juices in the bowl. Roast for 30 to 40 minutes, flipping over halfway through, until nicely charred and tender.
3. To make the chickpeas: Pat the chickpeas dry and add them to the mixing bowl with the leftover harissa juices. Toss well. Pour onto a second baking tray and roast for 25 to 30 minutes, until crisp and golden, flipping over halfway through.
4. To make the dukkah: Add all the ingredients to the third tray and roast for 10 minutes, until fragrant, turning round halfway through. Cool for 5 minutes, then use a blender or pestle and mortar to blitz to a small crumb with some lumps.
5. To make the tahini dressing: In a small bowl, stir together all the ingredients; start with 2 tablespoons (28 ml) of water and add more as needed for a thin, smooth consistency. Season with salt and pepper.
6. To serve: Divide the grains between four bowls and top with the roasted vegetables and the crunchy chickpeas. Drizzle over the tahini sauce and sprinkle over the dukkah. Top with some fresh herbs and pomegranate.

(CONTINUED ON PAGE 99)

(CONTINUED FROM PAGE 97)

7. Once cool, store leftovers in sealed containers in the fridge for 2 to 3 days or freeze everything (minus the tahini sauce) for up to 1 month in the freezer. The dukkah will last in a sealed container at room temperature for 1 to 2 months.

SERVING SUGGESTIONS AND VARIATIONS

Use any vegetables you have for this meal; it's a great way to use up any leftover produce. I also like to add broccoli, tomatoes, mushrooms, or squash.

NOTES

Dukkah is typically an Egyptian and Middle Eastern condiment that is made of a mixture of dried herbs, nuts, and spices that are roasted and then ground down to a crumbly mix. It is great for adding tons of flavor and texture on top of salads, soups, inside sandwiches, and on top of nourish bowls!

MISO EGGPLANT, TOFU, AND BROCCOLINI BOWLS

Serves: 4 | Time: 20 minutes

These nourish bowls feature a delicious, tangy miso-sesame sauce and a rainbow of vegetables. Serve these with crispy golden tofu, sticky white rice, and fiery kimchi for a delicious meal that's ready in a hurry.

For the Miso Sauce
- 2 tablespoons (32 g) miso paste, such as brown rice miso
- 2 tablespoons (30 ml) sesame oil
- 2 tablespoons (30 ml) maple syrup
- 1 tablespoon (15 ml) tamari or soy sauce
- 2 tablespoons (28 ml) lemon juice
- ½–1 teaspoon sriracha hot sauce

For the Bowl
- 2 cups (350 g) cooked sticky white rice
- 2 tablespoons (30 ml) sesame or olive oil, divided
- 8 ounces (200 g) extra-firm tofu, cubed
- 1 medium eggplant, sliced into wedges
- 8 ounces (200 g) broccolini

To Serve
- ¼ cup (60 g) kimchi
- 1 avocado, peeled and sliced
- 2 tablespoons (16 g) sesame seeds
- Fresh cilantro or parsley
- Chopped scallion
- Lime wedges

1. To make the miso sauce: Add all the ingredients to a small jar with a lid. Secure the lid and shake to mix until smooth and emulsified.
2. Heat 1 tablespoon (15 ml) of sesame oil in a large frying pan or wok over high heat. Once hot, add tofu and fry for 5 to 10 minutes, until golden and crispy. Transfer the tofu to a medium bowl and keep warm.
3. In the same pan, add the remaining oil and the eggplant. Fry over medium-high heat for 5 minutes, turning often until starting to cook through. Add the broccolini and fry for another 5 minutes, until tender and starting to char.
4. Add the tofu back to the pan along with half of the miso sauce. Toss the ingredients well to evenly coat them with the sauce and heat through.
5. Divide the rice between four bowls or plates. Top with the vegetables and tofu. Add the kimchi, avocado, sesame seeds, herbs, scallion, and lime. Drizzle the remaining miso sauce on top.
6. Eat right away or store leftovers, once cool, in a sealed container in the fridge for 2 to 3 days. Eat cold or stir-fry again to warm through.

SERVING SUGGESTIONS AND VARIATIONS
- *As with most nourish bowls, you can play around with any vegetables you have. Try cauliflower instead of broccoli and add zucchini and mushrooms instead of the eggplant.*
- *If you don't have sticky white rice, any rice or grain will work here.*

SESAME-CHILE-GARLIC TOFU NOODLES

Serves: 4 | Time: 20 minutes

Noodles are a great midweek meal, and these sesame-chile-garlic tofu noodles are so much better than getting take-out. They take less than twenty minutes to make, are packed with fresh and vibrant vegetables and protein-rich tofu, all served with a sticky chile, garlic, and sesame dressing.

For the Sauce
- ¼ cup (60 ml) tamari soy sauce
- 3 cloves garlic, crushed
- ½–1 red chile, chopped small
- 1 tablespoon (15 ml) maple syrup
- 1 tablespoon (15 ml) sesame oil
- 1 teaspoon sriracha hot sauce
- 1 teaspoon mirin

For the Noodles
- 2 tablespoons (30 ml) sesame or olive oil, divided
- 8 ounces (200 g) extra-firm tofu
- 4 scallions
- 1 carrot, peeled
- 1 red bell pepper
- 4 ounces (100 g) broccoli
- 4 ounces (100 g) bean sprouts
- 8 ounces (200 g) dry soba or udon noodles

To Serve
- 2 tablespoons (16 g) black and/or white sesame seeds
- Chile flakes
- Sliced fresh red or green chile (optional)

1. To make the sauce: Add all the ingredients to a small bowl and whisk until combined.
2. Heat 1 tablespoon (15 ml) of oil in a large frying pan over medium-high heat. Slice the tofu widthways into 2 or 3 thinner strips, then slice into triangles. Add to the hot oil and fry over medium-high heat for 5 minutes, or until crispy and golden and flip over to cook on the second side. Once golden, pour 1 tablespoon (15 ml) of the prepared sauce over the tofu, allowing the sauce to sizzle and evenly coat the tofu. Remove from the heat and warm again just before serving, if needed.
3. Chop off the ends of the scallions, then slice into 2-inch (5-cm) sticks; include the green part, too. Slice the carrot, bell pepper, and broccoli into small pieces or matchsticks.
4. Heat 1 tablespoon (15 ml) of oil in a large wok or frying pan over high heat. Add the scallions, carrot, bell pepper, and broccoli. Stir-fry over high heat for 5 minutes, or until the vegetables are tender but still have some bite. Add the bean sprouts and fry for 2 to 3 minutes, until cooked through. Add 2 tablespoons (28 ml) of the prepared sauce and fry for 1 minute.
5. Meanwhile, cook the noodles according to the package instructions and rinse in cold water.
6. Pour the noodles into the pan with the vegetables along with most of the sauce. Toss well and fry for 2 minutes.
7. Divide between four bowls, top with the sticky tofu and remaining sauce. Sprinkle over the sesame seeds, chile flakes, and fresh chile (if using).
8. Eat right away or store leftovers in a sealed container in the fridge for 2 to 3 days.

SERVING SUGGESTIONS AND VARIATIONS
- *Use any vegetables, such as eggplants, zucchini, mushrooms, baby corn, or sugar snap peas.*
- *Instead of tofu, add some edamame beans to the frying vegetables as they cook.*

CASHEW-CAULIFLOWER
AND SPINACH DAHL

Serves: 4 | Time: 10 minutes prep plus 40 minutes cooking

Nothing beats a wholesome, cozy bowl of dahl on a chilly day. This one features warming spices and vibrant greens, topped with sticky-sweet, roasted cauliflower florets. I love to make this for family dinners and save some for the day after as it tastes even better as the flavors infuse. This recipe is packed with protein and fiber, and it's naturally gluten-free. It can easily be made nut-free, too (see note on page 106).

For the Cauliflower
- 1 medium-size cauliflower, chopped into florets (3 cups, or 400 g)
- 2 tablespoons (32 g) cashew butter
- 1 tablespoon (15 ml) tamari or soy sauce
- 1 tablespoon (15 ml) sesame oil

For the Dahl
- 2 tablespoons (30 ml) olive oil
- 1 white onion, small dice
- 4 cloves garlic, crushed
- 1-inch (2.5-cm) piece fresh ginger, peeled and grated
- 1 teaspoon ground cumin
- ½ teaspoon smoked paprika
- ½ teaspoon ground turmeric
- 1 teaspoon black mustard seeds
- 1 heaped cup (200 g) red lentils
- 1⅔ cups (400 g) strained toma-toes (tomato passata)
- 2 cups (480 ml) vegetable stock
- 1 tablespoon (15 ml) tamari
- 2 tablespoons (32 g) cashew butter
- Salt and pepper, to taste
- 2 tablespoons (28 ml) lime juice
- 1½ packed cups (60 g) baby spinach

To Serve
- 2 cups (350 g) cooked rice
- Toasted cashew nuts
- Dairy-free yogurt
- Chopped fresh cilantro

1. Preheat the oven to 350°F (180°C, or gas mark 4). Line a baking tray with parchment paper.
2. To make the cauliflower: Pour the cashew butter, tamari, and sesame oil into a large mixing bowl, and stir together until smooth. Add the cauliflower florets and toss well to coat the cauliflower pieces. Season with salt and pepper. Spread the cauliflower evenly on the baking tray. Bake for 30 minutes, flipping over halfway through.
3. To make the dahl: Heat the olive oil in a large pan over high heat. Add the onion, garlic, and ginger. Fry for 5 minutes over high heat, until turning translucent. Add the cumin, smoked paprika, turmeric, and black mustard seeds. Continue to fry for 1 minute, or until fragrant.
4. Pour in the red lentils, strained tomatoes, stock, tamari, and cashew butter. Season with salt and pepper. Stir well and bring to a boil. Place a lid on the dahl and simmer over medium heat for 30 to 35 minutes, or until the lentils have softened. Stir the dahl every so often to prevent it from sticking to the bottom.

(CONTINUED ON PAGE 106)

(CONTINUED FROM PAGE 105)

5. Once the dahl is ready, add the lime juice to the pan along with the baby spinach. Stir well. Cook for 5 minutes, until the spinach leaves wilt.

6. Serve the dahl warm topped with the cashew roasted cauliflower, alongside rice, cashews, yogurt, and cilantro. Leftover dahl will keep in a sealed container in the fridge for 2 to 3 days or for up to 1 month in the freezer.

SERVING SUGGESTIONS AND VARIATIONS

- *Make this delicious dahl nut-free by using seed butter, such as tahini or sunflower seed butter, in place of the cashew butter.*
- *Batch cook this dahl as it tastes even better with time for the flavors to meld—great for meal prep and for popping in the freezer for a rainy day.*

MEXICAN JACKFRUIT-STUFFED SWEET POTATOES

Serves: 4 | Time: 10 minutes prep plus 60 minutes cooking

Jackfruit is such a versatile ingredient. If you've been converted and are looking for your next favorite way to use it, look no further than these Mexican-style stuffed sweet potatoes. Spiced with smoked paprika, cumin, and cilantro, this tomatoey jackfruit is vibrant and packed with goodness. Served in tender sweet potatoes, topped with fresh black bean and corn salsa, all drizzled with lime-yogurt, sour cream–style dressing, this is a supremely tasty and naturally gluten-free recipe.

For the Jackfruit
- 1 tablespoon (15 ml) olive oil
- 1 red onion, small dice
- 3 large cloves garlic, crushed
- 1 red bell pepper, small dice
- 1½ teaspoons hot smoked paprika
- ½ teaspoon ground cumin
- ¼ teaspoon ground coriander
- Salt and pepper, to taste
- 1 can jackfruit (drained: 10½ ounces, or 300 g)
- 1⅔ cups (400 g) strained tomatoes (tomato passata)
- 1 tablespoon (15 ml) tamari

For the Salsa
- 1 can sweet corn (drained: 1 cup, or 160 g)
- 1 can black beans (drained: 1½ cups, or 250 g)
- ½ cup (60 g) pomegranate
- 6 tablespoons (90 ml) lime juice, divided
- 2 tablespoons (2 g) chopped fresh cilantro

For the Bowl
- 4 medium sweet potatoes
- ½ cup (120 g) coconut yogurt
- 2 avocados
- Salt and pepper, to taste

1. Preheat the oven to 400°F (200°C, or gas mark 6) and puncture the potatoes all over with a knife. Place on a baking tray and bake for 45 to 60 minutes, or until crisp on the edges and tender inside.
2. Meanwhile, make the jackfruit: Place the jackfruit in a large bowl and break up the pieces with your hands. Heat the olive oil in a medium frying pan over high heat. Add the onion and garlic. Sauté for 5 minutes. Add the bell pepper and cook for 5 minutes, or until turning the onion is turning translucent.
3. Add the hot smoked paprika, cumin, cilantro, salt, and pepper. Fry for 1 minute, until fragrant. Pour in the jackfruit, tomato purée, and tamari. Stir well, bring to the boil, and reduce the heat to a medium simmer. Place a lid on and cook for 20 minutes, or until the jackfruit is tender and the sauce is thick.
4. While the jackfruit cooks, stir together the sweet corn, black beans, and pomegranate in a small bowl for the salsa. Add one-third of the lime juice, the cilantro, salt, and pepper. Toss well.
5. To make the dressing: In a small bowl, stir together the yogurt with one-third of the lime juice. Set it to one side.
6. Peel and de-stone the avocados and mash with a fork. Stir in the remaining lime juice with some salt and pepper.
7. When the potatoes are ready, slice each potato in half, leaving some of the potato intact. Fill the hole with the tomatoey jackfruit. Top with salsa, avocado, and dressing.
8. Once cool, all the components will last in separate sealed containers in the fridge for 2 to 3 days. Reheat leftovers in the microwave or on the stove. The jackfruit will keep well in the freezer for up to 1 month.

(CONTINUED ON PAGE 109)

(CONTINUED FROM PAGE 107)

SERVING SUGGESTIONS AND VARIATIONS

- *This tomatoey Mexican jackfruit is also great served over rice with the salsa, guacamole, and yogurt dressing. Or why not try this meal with regular baked potatoes, too?*
- *If you're a cheese lover, a sprinkling of vegan cheese on top is delicious.*

GARLICKY ROASTED VEGETABLE BASIL PASTA

Serves: 4 | Time: 5 minutes prep time plus 30 minutes cooking time

Being half-Italian, pasta has been a big part of my life. This is one of those pasta dishes that my family comes back to time and time again: it's fresh and vibrant, warming, and wholesome. Even better: you can pop the vegetables in the oven to bake while the pasta cooks. The sauce is something special: simply mash up the burst, juicy, roasted tomatoes with the soft sweet garlic—that's all there is to it.

For the Roasted Vegetables
- 2 zucchinis
- 2 bell peppers (any color)
- 3 cups (450 g) cherry tomatoes
- 4 cloves garlic, whole
- 3 tablespoons (45 ml) olive oil, divided
- 2 tablespoons (28 ml) balsamic vinegar
- 1 teaspoon dried basil
- 1 teaspoon dried oregano
- Salt and pepper, to taste

To Serve
- 2¼ cups (240 g) dry pasta, such as fusilli, penne, rigatoni
- 2 tablespoons (6 g) chopped fresh basil, plus extra to serve
- Chile flakes
- Homemade Vegan Parmesan (optional; page 167)

1. Preheat the oven to 350°F (180°C, or gas mark 4). Line two baking sheets with parchment paper.
2. Slice the zucchinis into half-moons, then slice the peppers into thin strips and in half lengthways. Add to a large mixing bowl with the tomatoes and whole garlic. Pour in 2 tablespoons (30 ml) of olive oil, balsamic vinegar, basil, oregano, salt, and pepper. Toss well.
3. To one baking sheet, add the zucchini and pepper. Add the tomatoes and garlic to the second sheet. Roast in the oven for 30 minutes, or until tender and the tomatoes have burst.
4. Meanwhile, cook the pasta according to the package instructions and drain. Set to one side.
5. Carefully pick out the garlic from the tray and gently squeeze out the garlic from the bulbs—it will be sticky. Squeeze into the pasta cooking pot along with the tomatoes, and 1 tablespoon (15 ml) of olive oil. Roughly mash the tomatoes and garlic together with a spoon to release their juices.
6. Add the pasta to the pot with the roasted vegetables and fresh basil. Toss well and serve with basil, chile flakes, and vegan parmesan (if using).
7. Enjoy this pasta warm or cold. Store leftovers in a sealed container in the fridge for 2 to 3 days. To reheat, warm slowly with a splash of water on the stove.

SERVING SUGGESTIONS AND VARIATIONS
To roast a whole garlic clove, peel away the excess from the garlic bulb and carefully slice off the very top, leaving the cloves together. Rub the top with 1 teaspoon of olive oil, salt, and pepper. Wrap in tinfoil. Roast at 350°F (180°C, or gas mark 4) for 40 minutes, or until tender. Store leftover garlic in a sealed container in the fridge for 1 week.

5

SNACKS

Never underestimate the power of a good snack. Whether it is a midmorning treat with a coffee or an afternoon pick-me-up to see you through the workday, these snacks will be sure to keep you going. With a mix of sweet and savory snacks, these all pack a nutritional and nourishing punch while tasting delicious.

Many recipes, such as my Easy Vegan Protein Balls (Six Ways) (page 129) and No-Bake Chocolate-Covered Muesli Bars (page 117) are great to meal prep on weekends for busy weeks. Or if you've got some time to spare, try my fluffy Cheesy Pesto and Sun-Dried Tomato Rolls (page 123).

You also will find daily essentials to fill your fridge and pantry, such as the best Homemade Super Seedy Crackers (page 119) and the creamiest Garlic-Herb Cashew Cheese (page 135). They are great for one or for when you are feeding a crowd.

CHOCOLATE FRUIT-AND-NUT FUDGE CUPS

Serves: 10 | Time: 20 minutes plus chilling

These little beauties were inspired by fruit-and-nut chocolate bars. I also love all things fudge so I combined the two in these decadent yet healthy, vegan, gluten-free fudge cups. Make these rich, double-layered fudge bites into whatever shapes you like. They are great for desserts, and you will be popping into the fridge for another one!

For the Chocolate Layer
- 5 ounces (140 g) dairy-free dark chocolate, broken up
- ¼ cup (60 g) almond butter or another nut/seed butter
- 3 tablespoons (45 g) coconut oil or coconut butter
- 1 teaspoon maple syrup
- A pinch of salt

For the Nut Butter Layer
- ⅔ cup (160 g) almond butter or another nut/seed butter
- ¼ cup (50 g) coconut oil or coconut butter
- 2 tablespoons (30 ml) maple syrup
- 1 teaspoon vanilla extract
- A pinch of salt

For Topping
- ¼ cup (30 g) raisins and/or dried cranberries
- ¼ cup (25 g) chopped pecans and/or pistachios

1. Arrange ten silicone cupcake molds on a tray or plate, or place ten regular cases into a cupcake tray.
2. To make the chocolate layer: Add all the ingredients to a small saucepan and gently heat the pan over low heat; allow the chocolate to melt and the mixture to become smooth. Stir regularly, until the chocolate is thick and glossy.
3. Divide the chocolate mixture between the ten cases and place in the freezer for 20 minutes to set. They will be almost fully set; that's okay. This is important so the two layers do not mix.
4. To make the nut butter layer: This layer requires less heat because the ingredients are naturally more liquid. I microwave them in a microwave-safe bowl in 10-second increments to melt the coconut oil, then whisk until smooth. Alternatively, place all the ingredients in a small saucepan as above and melt, whisking until smooth.
5. Remove the cups from the freezer and pour over the nut butter layer. Sprinkle over the dried fruits and nuts.
6. Chill again in the freezer for 1 hour, or until set. Store the fudge cups in a sealed container in the fridge for up to 1 week or in the freezer for up to 1 month.

SERVING SUGGESTIONS AND VARIATIONS
- *Make these fudge cups with any nut or seed butter you like; smooth and runny brands work best. You can also use any dried fruits and nuts for the topping, too.*
- *Keep these nut-free by using seed butter, such as tahini or sunflower seed butter, and using seeds or more dried fruits instead of the nuts on top.*

NO-BAKE CHOCOLATE-COVERED MUESLI BARS

Serves: 16 | Time: 20 minutes plus chilling

My dad took one of these bars to work with him every day for about two weeks after testing the recipe for these snack bars! They are great on-the-go for quick snacks or for enjoying with a cup of tea midmorning, and they will see you through the week so are great for meal prepping. They are rich and chocolatey with a wholesome and healthy base of oats, nuts, and dried fruits.

For the Muesli Bars
- 2 cups (200 g) oats
- ½ cup (80 g) roughly chopped almonds
- 1 cup (240 g) smooth almond butter
- ⅔ cup (160 ml) maple syrup
- 1½ tablespoons (21 g) coconut oil, melted
- 1 teaspoon vanilla extract
- A pinch of salt
- ½ cup (80 g) raisins or dried cranberries

For the Topping
- 7 ounces (200 g) dark chocolate, broken up
- 1½ tablespoons (21 g) coconut oil
- 1–2 tablespoons (16–32 g) smooth almond butter

1. Add the oats and almonds to a large frying pan. Fry them over high heat for about 5 minutes, until smelling toasty and turning golden. Remove from the heat. Line an 8-inch (20-cm) square dish (or equivalent) with parchment paper.
2. In a large mixing bowl, stir together the almond butter, maple syrup, melted coconut oil, vanilla, and salt. Whisk the mixture until silky smooth.
3. Add the oats, almonds, and dried fruits. Stir to a sticky mixture, then transfer to the lined dish. Press down firmly with the back of a spoon or spatula to make an even base. Place in the freezer for 10 minutes to set.
4. Meanwhile, melt the chocolate and coconut together in the microwave or over a bain-marie, ensuring the bottom of the pan doesn't touch the water.
5. Remove the muesli bars from the freezer and pour over the chocolate. Allow the chocolate to evenly cover the base, then drizzle over the almond butter. Use a knife or cocktail stick to swirl the almond butter into patterns.
6. Return the bars to the freezer for 30 minutes or in the fridge for 1 to 2 hours to set.
7. Once firm, use a sharp hot knife to carefully slice the muesli bars into sixteen pieces.
8. Eat right away or keep the bars in a sealed container in the fridge for up to 1 week or in the freezer for up to 1 month.

SERVING SUGGESTIONS AND VARIATIONS
- *To make these bars nut-free, swap the almond butter for a seed butter, such as tahini or sunflower seed butter, and swap the almonds for seeds.*
- *There are endless possibilities for these bars so play around with the nuts and dried fruits to use what you have at home. Try macadamia and cranberries, walnuts and dried apricots, or hazelnuts and chopped dates.*

HOMEMADE SUPER SEEDY CRACKERS

Makes: about 32 crackers | Time: 60 minutes

I used to think that making crackers at home involved lots of ingredients and that they'd never be as crisp as I wanted them to be. These Super Seedy Crackers proved me wrong. I am still amazed that they are only made with seeds plus seasoning, meaning that there is no flour. And they are just so easy. We love to snack on them as they are or dip them into Roasted Red Pepper Dip (page 79) and Hummus (page 69).

For the Crackers
- ⅓ cup (60 g) whole flaxseed
- ½ cup (80 g) whole chia seeds
- ½ cup (60 g) pumpkin seeds
- ½ cup (60 g) sunflower seeds
- 2 tablespoons (14 g) hemp seeds
- 2 tablespoons (18 g) ground chia or flaxseed
- 2 tablespoons (10 g) nutritional yeast
- 1 teaspoon salt
- 1 teaspoon mixed dried herbs
- ½ teaspoon garlic granules
- ¼ teaspoon chile flakes
- Black pepper
- 1 cup (240 ml) water

1. Add all of the seeds and seasonings to a large mixing bowl and stir together. Pour in the water, stir well, and allow to rest for 10 minutes. In this time, the chia or flaxseed will absorb all the liquid and form a sticky, gloopy mix.
2. Meanwhile, preheat the oven to 350°F (180°C, or gas mark 4). Line two baking sheets with parchment paper.
3. Divide the seed mix into two and place onto the two baking trays. Use a spatula to spread out the mixture to a large rectangle shape, about ½-inch (1 cm) thick or less. Ensure it is compact and flat. Make the edges as straight as possible for the neatest crackers.
4. Bake for 25 minutes, swapping the trays round to cook evenly. Remove from the oven, but leave the oven on. Carefully slice each tray of crackers into sixteen squares (or similar).
5. Flip all the crackers upside down. Bake for 30 minutes, moving the crackers round if the edges are crisping more than the middle. The crackers will be crispy, golden at the edges, and feel dry.
6. Allow to cool fully before eating. Store leftovers in a sealed container at room temperature for up to 1 week.

SERVING SUGGESTIONS AND VARIATIONS
- *Play around with the flavor of these crackers. Ground cumin or smoked paprika would be delicious.*
- *If the crackers do start to feel less crisp, simple bake them again for 10 minutes, or until crisping up.*

TWO-INGREDIENT FLATBREADS

Serves: 8 | Time: 20 minutes plus resting

These amazing, no yeast flatbreads were a revelation to me, and I have never looked back. Thick, fluffy, and deliciously chewy golden flatbreads made in two minutes with no kneading, proofing, or yeast required. They work every time and are easily gluten-free, making them a fantastic addition to Falafel Feast Bowls (page 69) or for dipping into hummus or soup.

For the Flatbreads
- 1 cup (240 g) thick, dairy-free yogurt
- 1¾ cups (245 g) self-raising flour or gluten-free self-raising flour, plus extra for dusting
- Salt
- Olive oil, for brushing

For Topping
- 1 tablespoon (14 g) vegan butter, melted
- 1 tablespoon (3 g) chopped fresh chives
- ½–1 teaspoon sesame seeds
- ¼–½ teaspoon chile flakes

1. Stir together the yogurt, flour, and a pinch of salt in a large mixing bowl to reach a shaggy dough. Place the dough a floured surface and with your hands bring to a smooth ball of dough. Return it to the bowl and cover. Leave for 20 minutes.
2. Divide the dough into eight pieces and roll into balls. Place each ball on a greased piece of parchment paper; the parchment is to help you avoid adding much extra flour as you handle the dough (which could dry out the flatbreads). Grease a rolling pin or lightly dust it with flour. Roll out each flatbread to the size of your hand.
3. Heat a large, nonstick pan or two pans if you want to make two at a time. Lightly grease the tops of the flatbreads with oil. Invert the flatbreads onto the hot pan(s). Fry for 2 to 3 minutes, until puffed up and the underneath is golden and starting to char. Flip over and fry off the second side.
4. Repeat to make all eight flatbreads, keeping them warm under a tea towel.
5. If desired, brush with melted butter and a sprinkling of chives, sesame seeds, and chile flakes.

SERVING SUGGESTIONS AND VARIATIONS
- *These flatbreads are easily gluten-free if you swap the flour for a gluten-free blend and skip the resting process. You have to work more carefully with the dough, but they puff up nicely!*
- *I love to serve these flatbreads with my Falafel Feast (page 69), and Roasted Red Pepper Dip (page 79), and My Favorite Minestrone Soup (page 63).*

CHEESY PESTO AND
SUN-DRIED TOMATO ROLLS

Serves: 12 | Time: 1 hour 30 minutes plus 1 hour 30 minutes proofing

When I make these fluffy, savory buns, I just cannot stop eating them. They have a light and pillowy-soft dough spread with a delicious, nut-free, homemade basil-spinach pesto, rich sun-dried tomatoes, and melting dairy-free cheese. These rolls are a great afternoon snack or a welcome addition to picnic, potlucks, and BBQs—any occasion where you can tear and share.

For the Pesto
- ½ cup (80 g) pumpkin seeds
- 2 tablespoons (10 g) nutritional yeast or Homemade Vegan Parmesan (page 167)
- 1 clove garlic, crushed
- 1 cup loosely packed (20 g) basil (small stems and leaves)
- ½ cup packed (20 g) baby spinach
- 2 tablespoons (28 ml) lemon juice
- 2 tablespoons (30 ml) olive oil
- Salt and pepper, to taste

For the Dough
- 1 cup (240 ml) unsweetened plant-based milk
- ¼ cup (56 g) vegan butter
- 2 tablespoons (18 g) ground chia or flaxseed, plus 5 tablespoons (74 ml) water
- 3¼ cups (455 g) all-purpose flour, divided
- 2 tablespoons (24 g) caster sugar
- 1 package (2¼ teaspoons, or 7 g) fast-acting yeast
- 1 teaspoon salt

For the Filling
- ⅔ cup (150 g) pesto (as above)
- ½ cup (90 g) chopped sun-dried tomatoes
- ⅔ cup (80 g) grated dairy-free cheese
- 1–2 tablespoons (15–30 ml) olive oil, for brushing
- Fresh basil leaves, to serve

1. If using store-bought pesto, skip ahead to step 3. To make the pesto: Preheat the oven to 350°F (180°C, or gas mark 4) and pour the pumpkin seeds onto a baking tray. Bake for 10 minutes, turning halfway through, until smelling toasty. Allow to cool fully.
2. Add the pumpkin seeds to a food processor with the nutritional yeast and garlic and blitz to a fine crumb. Add the basil, spinach, lemon, salt, and pepper. Blitz until chunky. Gradually pour in the olive oil while the machine is running, to reach a creamy consistency. Store in a sealed container in the fridge for up to 1 week.
3. To make the dough: Warm together the milk and butter in a small saucepan over low heat until just melted. Allow to cool slightly to lukewarm.
4. Stir together the chia seeds and water and leave for 5 minutes to form a gloopy mix. Whisk into the milk.

(CONTINUED ON PAGE 124)

(CONTINUED FROM PAGE 123)

5. Into a large mixing bowl or freestanding mixer with a dough hook attached, mix 3 cups (420 g) of flour, the sugar, yeast, and salt. Gradually pour in the milky mixture and bring to a rough dough. If using a machine, knead the dough on a low setting for 5 to 7 minutes, adding tablespoons of the extra ¼ cup (35 g) flour as needed. The dough will be smooth, shiny, and pulling away from the sides when it is ready. By hand, place the dough on a lightly floured surface and knead for 7 to 10 minutes, adding flour as needed.

6. Lightly grease a large bowl and place the dough inside. Cover loosely and leave somewhere warm for 1 hour, or until doubled in size.

7. When risen, punch down the dough and place it on a floured surface. Use a floured rolling pin to roll the dough to a rectangle 18 x 12 inches (46 x 30 cm). Spread with ⅔ cup (150 g) of the pesto, leaving a small border around the edge.

8. Sprinkle over the sun-dried tomatoes and cheese. Use the long edge to tightly and carefully roll up the dough into a log-shape, sealing in the edge. Trim off the edges and use a sharp knife or piece of cotton/floss to slice into twelve rolls (1½ inch, or 4 cm each).

9. Grease a 9- x 13-inch (23- x 33-cm) dish and place in the rolls, side by side so they lightly touch. Cover again and leave somewhere warm to proof for a second time for 30 minutes. They will rise to fill most of the dish.

10. Preheat the oven to 350°F (180°C, or gas mark 4). Brush the rolls with olive oil. Bake the rolls for 20 to 25 minutes, until golden on top and fluffy inside.

11. Enjoy warm, or allow to cool and top with fresh basil. Store leftover rolls in a sealed container at room temperature for 2 to 3 days or in the fridge for 3 to 4 days. Freeze the rolls for up to 1 month; defrost at room temperature.

SERVING SUGGESTIONS AND VARIATIONS
- *You can also use store-bought pesto for these rolls.*
- *I love to brush the rolls with the oil from a jar of sun-dried tomatoes for extra flavor.*

BLUEBERRY WAGON WHEELS

Serves: 12 | Time: 40 minutes plus chilling and cooling time

I cannot remember a time without wagon wheels, the soft biscuit covered with a sticky jam layer and fluffy marshmallow all enrobed in a thick layer of chocolate . . . so I simply had to include a homemade plant-based version in the book. This wagon wheel has had a bit of a health boost—featuring an oaty biscuit, homemade berry-chia jam, and whipped coconut fluff—and they are even better than I remember. They also soften over time, so they only get more delicious.

For the Cookies
- 3 tablespoons (45 ml) maple syrup
- 3 tablespoons (45 g) smooth cashew or almond butter
- 2 tablespoons (18 g) coconut sugar
- ½ teaspoon vanilla extract
- ½ cup (50 g) oat flour
- ½ cup (70 g) all-purpose or gluten-free flour
- ½ teaspoon baking powder
- A pinch of salt

For the Blueberry Chia Jam
- 1 cup (125 g) fresh blueberries
- 1 tablespoon (11 g) chia seeds

For the Coconut Fluff
- ½ cup (120 g) thick coconut yogurt or cream (see tip)
- ¾ cup (60 g) dried coconut
- 1 tablespoon (14 g) coconut oil, softened

For the Chocolate
- 7 ounces (200 g) dark chocolate, broken up
- 1 tablespoon (14 g) coconut oil
- 1 ounces (30 g) white chocolate
- 1 tablespoon (5 g) dried coconut

1. To make the cookies: In a large bowl, stir together the maple syrup, nut butter, sugar, and vanilla until smooth. Add the flours, baking powder, and salt. Stir to a smooth and thick cookie dough; it may be crumbly so bring it together with your hands and shape into a ball. Wrap in plastic wrap and chill in the fridge for 20 minutes.

2. Meanwhile, preheat the oven to 350°F (180°C, or gas mark 4). Line two baking sheets with parchment paper.

3. Between two pieces of parchment paper, carefully roll out the cookie dough to ½-inch (1-cm) thickness; it may crack at the edges; push it back together with your fingers. Use a 2-inch (5-cm) circle cookie cutter to cut out the cookies; reroll the dough as needed. You will have twenty-four cookies. Place the cookies onto the baking sheets; they do not spread a lot. Place back in the fridge for 5 minutes; this helps the cookies retain their shape.

4. Bake the cookies for 10 minutes, until golden and crisp, turning the baking sheets halfway through. Allow to cool fully; this should take 30 to 60 minutes.

5. To make the blueberry chia jam: Blitz the blueberries in a blender until smooth. Stir in the chia seeds. Set it aside for 30 minutes to form a gel.

6. To make the coconut fluff: To a clean blender, add all the ingredients and blend until thick and combined.

7. To assemble the wagon wheels: Place half of the cookies upside down and spread these with a thick layer of coconut fluff. Top with a small spoonful of jam. Sandwich the filling together by placing on a second cookie and pressing down. I like to fill in the edges and gaps with extra coconut fluff so that no jam pokes out the sides. Repeat to make twelve sandwiches.

(CONTINUED ON PAGE 128)

(CONTINUED FROM PAGE 127)

8. Place the cookie sandwiches in the fridge. Cover a plate with parchment paper. Melt together the chocolate and coconut oil in the microwave or on the stove, until smooth and glossy.

9. Place the chocolate in a shallow bowl. Dip each sandwich cookie in the chocolate to cover the base and sides. Then, place the cookie on a fork over the bowl and spoon over the chocolate to cover the top. Fill in any gaps and allow excess chocolate to drip off.

10. Transfer to parchment-covered plate. Repeat to cover all twelve sandwiches. Chill in the fridge for 10 minutes to set the chocolate.

11. Melt the white chocolate, decorate the blueberry wagon wheels with patterns, and top with dried coconut.

12. Keep the wagon wheels in a sealed container in the fridge for 5 to 7 days; they will soften over time but retain their bite!

SERVING SUGGESTIONS AND VARIATIONS

Coconut cream is the thick part of coconut milk. Place a can of full-fat coconut milk in the fridge overnight, then scoop off the solid cream part. Save the water for smoothies and oatmeal (pages 17 and 19).

EASY VEGAN PROTEIN BALLS (SIX WAYS)

Serves: 8 | Time: 10 minutes plus chilling

These protein balls are so easy to make, you will never have to do with store-bought again. With a five-ingredient base recipe and any number of add-ins, they are ready in ten minutes in one bowl. And they are fully vegan, gluten-free, and high in protein—which one will be your favorite? Follow the base recipe, then add the ingredients for each flavor you'd like to make. (Note which nut or seed butter is specified and if you need to change the flavor of the protein powder, too.)

For the Base Recipe
- ½ cup (120 g) runny, smooth nut or seed butter
- 2–3 tablespoons (30–45 ml) maple syrup
- 1 tablespoon (9 g) ground chia or flaxseed
- ½ cup (50 g) oat flour
- 2 tablespoons (20 g) vegan vanilla or other protein powder or more oat flour
- A pinch of salt

Chocolate Chip
- Use peanut butter
- ¼ cup (40 g) dairy-free chocolate chips

Almond Coconut Chocolate
- Use almond butter
- 2 tablespoons (8 g) dried coconut, plus extra
- 2 tablespoons (20 g) dairy-free dark chocolate chips
- 8 whole almonds

White Chocolate Macadamia
- Use almond or cashew butter
- ¼ cup (40 g) chopped macadamia, plus extra for topping
- 2 tablespoons (20 g) dairy-free white chocolate chips

Cinnamon Oatmeal Raisin
- Use almond butter
- ½ teaspoon ground cinnamon
- ¼ cup (40 g) raisins

Tahini Pistachio
- Use tahini
- 2 tablespoons (20 g) crushed pistachios

Chocolate Hazelnut
- Use peanut butter
- Use vegan chocolate-flavored protein
- 16 whole hazelnuts
- 2 tablespoons (20 g) dairy-free, dark chocolate chips

1. To make the base recipe: Line a large baking tray with parchment paper. Use the nut/seed butter and protein powder specified. Combine the base ingredients in a large bowl. The mixture will be firm but soft enough.
2. To make the chocolate chip: Add the chocolate chips, roll into eight balls and chill in the fridge for 20 minutes.
3. To make the almond coconut chocolate: Add the dried coconut and roll into eight balls. Chill in the fridge for 10 minutes. Melt the chocolate and dip each ball into the chocolate. Top with an almond and extra coconut; chill in the fridge for 10 minutes.

(CONTINUED ON PAGE 131)

(CONTINUED FROM PAGE 129)

4. To make the white chocolate macadamia: Fold in the macadamia nuts, roll into eight balls and chill in the fridge for 10 minutes. Melt the white chocolate and dip each ball into the chocolate. Top with extra macadamia; chill in the fridge for 10 minutes.

5. To make the cinnamon oatmeal raisin: Stir in the cinnamon and raisins. Roll into eight balls; chill in the fridge for 10 minutes.

6. To make the tahini pistachio: Roll into eight balls. Set in the freezer for 10 minutes (this variation is softer). Then roll in the crushed pistachios. Chill in the fridge for 10 minutes.

7. To make the chocolate hazelnut: Divide the mixture into eight balls. Make an indent into each ball with your thumb and place a hazelnut inside. Roll the mixture around the nut and repeat to make eight balls. Chill in the fridge and melt the chocolate. Slice the remaining hazelnuts in half. Dip each ball in the chocolate and top with two hazelnut halves. Set in the fridge for 10 minutes.

8. These will keep well in a sealed container in the fridge for at least 1 week; freeze them for up to 1 month.

SERVING SUGGESTIONS AND VARIATIONS

Play around with other flavors by changing the type of nut/seed butter and the protein flavor. Choose other add-ins, too, like other nuts, seeds, or dried fruits!

SUN-DRIED TOMATO
AND OLIVE CHEESE SCONES

Serves: 10 | Time: 30 minutes

Savory scones were a revelation to me. The comforting cheese, sun-dried tomato and olive flavors, they all work so well in a fluffy and golden scone. These are similar to savory breakfast biscuits: a crisp golden outside, a fluffy tender inside packed with Mediterranean flavors, and a cheesy top.

For the Scones
- 2½ cups (350 g) all-purpose flour, plus extra for dusting
- 2 tablespoons (10 g) nutritional yeast
- 4 teaspoons (18 g) baking powder
- ½ teaspoon salt
- ¼ cup (56 g) vegan butter or margarine, cubed
- ¾ cup (180 ml) unsweetened plant-based milk
- ½ cup (60 g) grated vegan cheese, plus extra for topping
- ⅓ cup (60 g) chopped sun-dried tomatoes
- ⅓ cup (60 g) chopped olives
- 1 tablespoon (15 ml) olive oil, for brushing

To Serve
- Garlic-Herb Cashew Cheese (page 135)

1. Preheat the oven to 410°F (210°C, or gas mark 6 to 7). Line two baking trays with parchment paper.
2. Add the flour, nutritional yeast, baking powder, and salt to a large bowl. Stir well. Add the vegan butter, and use a knife to cut the fat into the flour.
3. Use your fingers to rub the mixture to form a crumbly mix.
4. Make a well in the middle and pour in the milk, cheese, sun-dried tomatoes, and olives. Use a spoon to stir the mixture together to a sticky ball.
5. Pour the scone mixture onto a lightly floured surface and knead lightly for 1 minute to form a smooth ball of dough.
6. Roll the dough out until it is 1-inch (2½-cm) thick. Use a 2-inch (5-cm) round cookie cutter to cut out ten scones, re-rolling the dough as needed to use it all up.
7. Arrange the scones on the trays. Brush with olive oil and sprinkle over extra cheese.
8. Bake for 15 minutes, turning the trays halfway through. The scones will be golden, risen, and crisp at the edges when they are ready. Cool on a wire rack. Enjoy these warm or cold.
9. Once cool, store the scones in a sealed container at room temperature for 2 to 3 days or in the fridge, if it is warm. Scones can also be frozen for up to 1 month; defrost at room temperature.

SERVING SUGGESTIONS AND VARIATIONS
If you don't like olives, swap these for extra sun-dried tomatoes. Feel free to add ½ teaspoon of mixed dried herbs to the mix, too.

GARLIC-HERB CASHEW CHEESE

Serves: 8 | Time: 20 minutes plus overnight soaking and chilling

This cheese was a long work in progress, but I am finally there. This is the perfect cashew cheese: firm enough to serve as a cheese ball, soft and creamy enough to spread onto crackers. Flavored with garlic, fresh basil, thyme, and oregano, it packs a punch. And it is made from simple ingredients in only a few steps—with no cheese cloth needed!

For the Cheese
- 1 cup (140 g) cashews
- 2 tablespoons (10 g) nutritional yeast
- 2 tablespoons (28 ml) lemon juice
- 2 tablespoons (28 ml) water
- 1 teaspoon apple cider vinegar or white wine vinegar
- 1 clove garlic, crushed
- ½ teaspoon garlic granules
- 1 teaspoon salt
- Black pepper, to taste
- ½ teaspoon chopped fresh basil
- ½ teaspoon chopped fresh thyme
- ½ teaspoon chopped fresh oregano

To Serve
- Fresh herbs
- Chile flakes
- Homemade Seedy Crackers (page 119)

1. Place the cashews in a large bowl. Either cover with water and leave overnight to soak, or cover with boiling water and let soak for 1 hour. Drain and rinse the soaked cashews.
2. Pour the cashews into a food processor or high-speed blender with the nutritional yeast, lemon juice, water, vinegar, garlic, garlic granules, salt, and pepper. Blend until really smooth, scraping down the sides as needed. Continue blending until no lumps remain.
3. Stir in the fresh herbs.
4. Line a small bowl or ramekin with plastic wrap so it overhangs the edges. Pour in the cashew cheese and smooth over the top. Bring together the edges of plastic wrap and tightly twist at the top to seal in all the cheese. Let it firm up in the fridge overnight.
5. Once firm, untie the plastic wrap. Invert the cheese onto a plate; it will be firm but delicate, so be careful. Sprinkle with herbs and chile flakes.
6. Store the tightly wrapped cheese in the fridge for up to 1 week. Freeze for up to 1 month; defrost in the fridge overnight.

SERVING SUGGESTIONS AND VARIATIONS
Other herbs will work well here, such as fresh chives, mint, or even parsley.

6
SWEETS

Baking has been close to my heart from a young age, and I have such fond memories of spending time in the kitchen making chocolate chip cookies and apple pies. Plant-based sweets have opened my eyes to how versatile and exciting vegan can be, and you don't need a cupboard full of weird and wonderful ingredients to turn out something fabulous.

In fact, the recipes in this chapter, like elsewhere, focus on simple, easy-to-find ingredients, often with healthier twists, too. Perhaps the most-loved recipe here is my Single-Serve Cookie (Four Ways) (page 143) as it's perfect for a quick dessert for one and will please just about anyone who takes a bite. For a showstopper dessert, the Orange-Cardamom Layer Cake (page 145) is sure to impress, while the Apple-and-Blackberry Crumble Pie (page 157) is a simply wonderful, nostalgic dessert that will take you right back to your childhood!

FUDGY RASPBERRY BROWNIES

Serves: 16 | Time: 5 minutes prep plus 30 minutes baking

I have a secret: these brownies are actually healthy! They are made with plant-based whole foods, but they taste just as indulgent, rich, and fudgy as regular brownies. The pop of the raspberries adds a fruity twist to these chocolatey squares that just get better and better. Plus, they are easily gluten-free and come together in one bowl—which you will be licking clean!

For the Brownies
- 1 cup (200 g) applesauce or apple purée
- ½ cup (120 g) runny, cashew or almond butter
- ⅔ cup (160 ml) maple syrup
- 2 tablespoons (30 ml) melted coconut oil
- 1 teaspoon vanilla extract
- ¾ cup (105 g) all-purpose or gluten-free flour
- ½ cup (40 g) cacao or cocoa powder
- 1 teaspoon ground coffee
- 1 teaspoon baking powder
- A pinch of salt
- 16 raspberries
- 4 ounces (110 g) dairy-free chocolate, chopped

1. Preheat the oven to 350°F (180°C, or gas mark 4). Line an 8-inch (20-cm) baking dish with parchment paper.
2. Add the applesauce, nut butter, maple syrup, coconut oil, and vanilla to a large mixing bowl. Whisk until smooth. Sift in the flour, cacao powder, coffee, baking powder, and salt. Whisk to a smooth batter with no lumps of flour.
3. Fold in most of the chocolate.
4. Pour into the lined dish and smooth over the top. Press in the raspberries and the remaining chocolate.
5. Bake for 28 to 32 minutes, or until an inserted skewer comes out mostly clean. The brownies will be firmer around the edges, but still slightly fudgy in the middle.
6. Cool for 20 minutes in the dish, then carefully lift out and cool on a wire rack.
7. Once cool, use a sharp hot knife to slice into sixteen brownies. Store the brownies in a sealed container in the fridge for 3 to 5 days or 1 to 2 days at room temperature. Freeze the brownies for up to 1 month.

SERVING SUGGESTIONS AND VARIATIONS
Swap the raspberries for any berries such as blueberries, blackberries, or strawberries. These also are great with chopped nuts folded though; try ½ cup (60–70 g) of chopped pecans or hazelnuts.

CHOCOLATE-ESPRESSO CARAMEL SLICES

Serves: 10 | Time: 20 minutes plus 1 to 2 hours chilling

If you love mocha, then you will love these. The coffee adds a delicious twist on the classic caramel millionaire slice, and of course it's made with plant-based ingredients as well. A no-bake, cacao-and-coffee biscuit base is topped with a thick layer of coffee salted caramel that's dipped in melted chocolate. They simply melt in your mouth!

For the Biscuit Base
- 1¼ cup (125 g) rolled oats
- ½ cup (70 g) ground almonds
- ½ cup (60 g) pecans
- 1 tablespoon (3 g) ground coffee
- 1 tablespoon (5 g) cacao or cocoa powder
- ¼ cup (60 g) cashew or almond butter
- 3 tablespoons (45 g) coconut oil, melted
- 2 tablespoons (30 ml) maple syrup
- A pinch of salt

For the Caramel
- ½ cup (120 g) cashew or almond butter
- ¼ cup plus 2 tablespoons (90 ml) maple syrup
- ¼ cup plus 1 tablespoon (75 ml) melted coconut oil
- 1 teaspoon coffee dissolved in 1 teaspoon hot water
- A pinch of salt

For the Topping
- 3 ounces (85 g) dairy-free chocolate, chopped
- Coffee beans
- Cacao nibs
- Flaky salt

1. Line an 8- x 4-inch (20- x 10-cm) loaf pan with parchment paper.
2. To make the base: Add the oats, almonds, pecans, and coffee to a food processor and blitz to a fine meal. Pour into a medium mixing bowl and add the cacao powder, cashew butter, melted coconut oil, maple syrup, and a pinch of salt. Stir to a sticky mix that holds together when pressed between your fingers.
3. Pour into the pan and press down firmly to form an even base biscuit layer. Chill in the fridge while you make the caramel.
4. To make the caramel: Add all the ingredients to a small bowl. Stir until smooth and silky. Pour over the base layer and chill in the fridge for 1 hour, or until set and firm to touch.
5. Remove the caramel slices from the pan and use a hot, sharp knife to slice into ten bars or squares. Pop the bars in the fridge while you prepare the toppings.
6. To make the topping: Line a baking tray with parchment paper. Melt the chocolate over a double boiler or bain-marie. One by one, dip each caramel slice into the chocolate and place on the tray. Sprinkle with coffee beans, cacao nibs, and flaky salt. Set in the fridge for 10 minutes, or until the chocolate has hardened.
7. Store the slices in a sealed container in the fridge for up to 1 week or in the freezer for up to 1 month.

SERVING SUGGESTIONS AND VARIATIONS
Make sure these are gluten-free by using gluten-free certified oats. Make these nut-free by swapping the ground almonds for extra oats, the pecans for seeds such as sunflower or pumpkin seeds, and swap and cashew/almond butter for a seed butter such as tahini.

SINGLE-SERVE COOKIE (FOUR WAYS)

Serves: 1 | Time: 10 minutes plus 15 minutes chilling

This cookie is here for you on those cold winter nights, lazy summer afternoons, or midmorning coffee breaks. We all have them: the times when you just need a cookie but don't want to make a dozen, so a single-serve cookie is the answer. This cookie is thick and chewy, buttery, and crisp on the outside and tender in the middle. Plus there are four options: classic chocolate chip, triple chocolate, funfettti, and fruit-and-nut.

For the Cookie Dough Base
- 2 tablespoons (28 g) vegan butter
- 2 tablespoons (20 g) light brown sugar
- ¼ teaspoon vanilla extract
- ¼ cup (35 g) all-purpose, gluten-free, or oat flour
- 1 teaspoon cornstarch
- ¼ teaspoon baking powder
- 1 teaspoon plant-based milk
- A pinch of salt

For the Triple Chocolate Cookie
- 1 teaspoon (3 g) cocoa powder (to replace 1 teaspoon of flour)
- 1 tablespoon (10 g) dairy-free dark chocolate chips
- 1 tablespoon (10 g) dairy-free white chocolate chips

For the Classic Chocolate Chip Cookie
- 2 tablespoons (10 g) dairy-free chocolate chips

For the Funfetti Cookie
- 1 tablespoon (12 g) funfetti sprinkles

For the Fruit-and-Nut Cookie
- 1 tablespoon (10 g) chopped dried fruit, such as raisins
- 1 tablespoon (10 g) chopped nuts, such as pistachios

1. Add the butter and sugar to a small mixing bowl and beat until smooth. Add the vanilla, flour, cornstarch, baking powder, milk, and salt. Stir to a thick dough; it will seem dry at first, but it will come together.
2. To make the triple chocolate cookie: Remove 1 teaspoon of the measured flour and replace with the cocoa powder. Stir to a cookie dough and fold in both chocolate chips.
3. To make the other cookies: Fold in the added ingredients to a sticky dough.
4. Bring the cookie dough to a ball and place it on a piece of parchment. Chill in the fridge for 10 to 15 minutes.
5. Meanwhile, preheat the oven to 400°F (200°C, or gas mark 6).
6. Place the cookie dough and parchment on a baking sheet. Press down slightly, and add a few chocolate chips or sprinkles or nuts on top. Bake for 10 to 12 minutes, until crisping at the edges.
7. Cool for 10 to 20 minutes on a cooling rack; the cookie will firm up as it cools. Enjoy right away or allow to cool completely. Store in a sealed container at room temperature for 3 to 5 days or in the freezer for up to 1 month.

SERVING SUGGESTIONS AND VARIATIONS
Try these with nut butter for a delicious nutty cookie.

NOTES
- *Note that the cookies do not spread so you will need to flatten them and that you may need 1 to 2 tablespoons (15 to 28 ml) more milk.*
- *These are great with oat flour. Note that ¼ cup of oat flour weighs 25 grams.*

ORANGE-CARDAMOM LAYER CAKE

Serves: 10 | Time: 40 minutes plus cooling

This cake tastes like summer. It's fresh, vibrant, and such an impressive dessert for friends and family. Three fluffy, orange-and-cardamom sponges sandwiched with a luscious orange-cardamom buttercream make one delicious showstopper.

For the Cake
- 2 oranges, zested
- ¾ cup (180 ml) orange juice (2 small oranges)
- ¾ cup (180 ml) sunflower oil
- ¾ cup (180 g) thick, dairy-free yogurt
- ½ cup (112 g) caster sugar
- 1½ teaspoons vanilla extract
- ¾ teaspoon ground cardamom
- 2½ cups plus 2 tablespoons (367 g) all-purpose flour
- 1 tablespoon (14 g) baking powder
- 1½ teaspoons baking soda
- A pinch of salt

For the Buttercream
- ¾ cup (170 g) vegan butter, softened
- 1 orange, zested
- 3 cups (480 g) confectioners' sugar
- 1 teaspoon vanilla extract
- 3 tablespoons (45 ml) plant-based milk
- ¼–½ teaspoon ground cardamom

For Decorating
- 3 slices of orange
- Edible flowers, optional

1. Preheat the oven to 350°F (180°C, or gas mark 4). Grease and line three 6-inch (15-cm) cake tins with parchment paper.
2. Add the zest to a large mixing bowl with the orange juice, sunflower oil, yogurt, caster sugar, vanilla, and cardamom. Whisk until smooth.
3. Sift in the flour, baking powder, and baking soda. Add the salt. Whisk to a thick batter with no specks of flour; be careful not to overmix. The batter is quite thick; this is normal.
4. Divide the batter equally between the three tins and smooth over the tops. Bake for 22 to 24 minutes, or until an inserted skewer comes out clean. They will be well risen and golden on top.
5. Cool for 10 minutes, then carefully remove from the tins to cool fully on a wire rack.
6. Once cool, slice off the tops or the cakes if they have domed so they are flat.
7. To make the buttercream: Add the softened butter to a large bowl and use a handheld electric or freestanding mixer to beat the butter until smooth. Gradually beat in the orange zest, confectioners' sugar, vanilla, milk, and cardamom. Once incorporated, continue to beat for 1 to 2 minutes, until fluffy.
8. To assemble the cake: Place one cake on a plate and spread evenly with buttercream. Repeat with the second cake and then top with the third sponge. Cover the sides and top with more buttercream. I like to use a tilted spatula and a smoothing scraper on a turntable.
9. Pipe any leftover buttercream on top, and decorate the cake with fresh orange slices and flowers (if using).
10. Leftover cake will keep in the fridge for 3 to 5 days, or keep unfrosted cake in the freezer for up to 1 month. Allow the sponges to defrost at room temperature before decorating.

SERVING SUGGESTIONS AND VARIATIONS
Make this into a two-tier cake using two 8-inch (20-cm) pans, baking for about 25 minutes.

LEMON-RASPBERRY
AND PISTACHIO LOAF CAKE

Serves: 8 to 10 | Time: 60 minutes plus cooling

Nothing lifts my mood more than a slice of cake, especially when it is vibrant, zesty, and fruity. Packed with fresh lemon, juicy raspberries, and thick vegan yogurt, this loaf cake is light, fluffy, and slightly green from the delicious pistachios. The nuts add a lovely flavor to the cake that will keep guests coming back for more.

For the Loaf Cake
- ½ cup (120 g) thick, dairy-free yogurt
- ½ cup (120 ml) plant-based milk
- 1 tablespoon (15 ml) lemon juice
- 2 tablespoons (30 ml) sunflower oil (or melted and cooled coconut oil)
- ½ cup (110 g) caster sugar
- 2 lemons, zested
- 1½ cups (210 g) plus 1 teaspoon all-purpose or gluten-free flour
- 1½ teaspoons baking powder
- ½ teaspoon baking soda
- ¾ cup (75 g) ground pistachios
- A pinch of salt
- 1 heaped cup (140 g) raspberries, plus a few extra

For the Frosting
- ¾ cup (180 g) thick, dairy-free yogurt
- Raspberries
- Pistachios

1. Preheat the oven to 350°F (180°C, or gas mark 4) with a rack in the center. Line a 9- x 5-inch (23- x 13-cm) loaf pan with parchment paper. Toss the raspberries with the 1 teaspoon of flour.
2. To a large mixing bowl, add the yogurt, milk, lemon juice, sunflower oil, caster sugar, and lemon zest. Whisk until smooth.
3. Sift in the flour, baking powder and baking soda. Add the pistachios and salt. Whisk to a smooth batter with no lumps. Fold in the floured raspberries; leave any extra flour behind. Transfer to the loaf pan.
4. Smooth over the top and add a few extra raspberries. Bake in the middle of the oven for 50 minutes, or until risen and golden and an inserted skewer comes out clean. If the cake is turning too dark, cover with foil after 35 minutes.
5. Allow the cake to cool for 10 minutes, then carefully lift out of the loaf pan to cool fully on a wire rack.
6. Once cool, spread the loaf with the yogurt and top with extra raspberries and pistachios.
7. Leftover cake will keep in a sealed container in the fridge for 3 to 5 days. You can freeze the unfrosted cake for up to 1 month. Defrost at room temperature, then decorate.

SERVING SUGGESTIONS AND VARIATIONS
- *Make your own ground pistachios by blitzing shelled, raw, unsalted pistachios in a blender to a fine meal—like ground almonds.*
- *To make this loaf cake gluten-free, use your preferred baking 1:1 gluten-free flour blend with xanthan gum to help bind the batter.*

BANOFFEE PIE JARS

Serves: 4 regular or 6 smaller jars | Time: 30 minutes plus cooling/chilling time

I am officially a huge fan of making my own salted caramel thanks to this recipe. Layered between a wholesome oat biscuit base, fluffy whipped cream, and slices of fresh banana, top these pie jars with shaved chocolate to make single-serve desserts of the much-loved British classic.

For the Biscuit Base
- 2 cups (200 g) oat flour
- 3 tablespoons (45 g) melted vegan butter or coconut oil
- 3 tablespoons (45 ml) maple syrup
- ½ teaspoon vanilla extract
- A pinch of salt

For the Salted Caramel
- 1 cup (160 g) light brown sugar
- ¼ cup (60 ml) water
- 2 cups (480 ml) full-fat coconut milk or single dairy-free cream
- ¼ cup (56 g) vegan butter, cubed
- A pinch of salt

For the Layers
- ¾ cup (180 ml) dairy-free whipping cream
- 2–3 bananas, sliced
- Shaved chocolate

1. To make the biscuit base: Preheat the oven to 350°F (180°C, or gas mark 4). Line a baking sheet with parchment paper. Stir together all the ingredients and crumble them into the sheet. Bake for 12 minutes, stirring halfway through. Allow to cool fully, about 1 hour.
2. To make the salted caramel: Add the sugar and water to a large saucepan; this expands a lot, so you need a large pan. Warm over high heat until the sugar dissolves, stirring often. Once smooth, allow it to bubble away over high heat for 3 minutes, until it is darker in color and thicker.
3. Meanwhile, gently warm the coconut milk until lukewarm.
4. Briefly remove the caramel from the heat and pour in the warmed coconut milk. Add the butter. Return the pan to a high heat and use a balloon whisk to stir the mixture constantly until the butter dissolves.
5. Allow to simmer again and continue to heat for 15 minutes, whisking often so the pan does not catch. The caramel is done when it has reduced by three to four times, and it is dark, glossy, and coming away from the edges of the pan. Whisk in the salt and remove from the heat.
6. Pour into a heat-proof container to cool for 1 hour before using. The caramel will thicken as it cools. If it cools too much, partially submerge the container into a pan of warm water.
7. Before assembling the jars, whip the cream until fluffy.
8. Divide the biscuit base between the glasses, top with whipped cream, caramel, and banana slices. Repeat the layers and finish with some chocolate.
9. Eat right away, or keep the desserts in their glasses, covered, in the fridge for 2 to 3 days.

SERVING SUGGESTIONS AND VARIATIONS
Make these desserts lighter by using thick Greek-style, dairy-free yogurt instead of whipped cream.

CHOCOLATE CHIP COOKIE LAYER CAKE

Makes: 10 regular or 20 mini cookies | Time: 15 minutes plus chilling

This cake is the dream for special occasions, birthdays, or for when the cake cravings kick in. It has two layers of light, fluffy, chocolate chip sponge sandwiched with luscious chocolate chip–vanilla buttercream, all coated with the best chocolate buttercream. The best way to top this cake is with these chewy, sweet, and golden chocolate chips cookies which are great on their own.

For the Chocolate Chip Cookies
- ¼ cup (56 g) vegan butter
- ½ cup (80 g) light brown sugar
- ¼ cup (50 g) caster sugar
- 2 teaspoons (10 ml) vanilla extract
- ¾ cup (105 g) all-purpose or gluten-free flour
- 1 teaspoon cornstarch
- ½ teaspoon baking soda
- 1 tablespoon (15 ml) plant-based milk
- A pinch of salt
- ½ cup (80 g) dairy-free chocolate chips

For the Cake
- ½ cup (120 ml) plant-based milk
- 1 tablespoon (15 ml) lemon juice or apple cider vinegar
- ⅓ cup (76 g) vegan butter, softened
- ½ cup (100 g) caster sugar
- ⅓ cup (84 g) applesauce
- 1 tablespoon (15 ml) vanilla extract
- 1½ cups (210 g) all-purpose flour
- 1 teaspoon baking powder
- ½ teaspoon baking soda
- A pinch of salt
- 3½ ounces (100 g) dairy-free chocolate chips

For the Buttercream
- 1 batch Vanilla Buttercream (page 185 [same as Red Velvet Cupcakes])
- 1 ounces (30 g) dairy-free chocolate chips
- 1 batch Chocolate Buttercream (page 185 [same as Red Velvet Cupcakes])

TO MAKE THE CHOCOLATE CHIP COOKIES
1. Add the vegan butter to a large mixing bowl with both sugars. Beat until smooth and creamy. Add the vanilla and beat again. Add the flour, cornstarch, baking soda, milk, and salt. Beat to a sticky, thick cookie dough. Fold in the chocolate chips.
2. For mini cookies, divide the cookie dough in twenty equal pieces for cookies as shown here, or for regular-sized cookies, divide the dough into ten pieces. Roll into balls, place on a baking sheet and chill in the fridge for 10 to 15 minutes.
3. Meanwhile, preheat the oven to 350°F (180°C, or gas mark 4). Space the cookie dough balls on a parchment-lined baking sheet; leave 2-inch (5-cm) gap round the cookies as they spread.
4. Bake mini cookies for 6 to 8 minutes or regular cookies for 7 to 10 minutes, or until crisping at the edges and the cookies have spread out.
5. Cool for 10 minutes on the baking sheets, then cool fully on a wire rack.

(CONTINUED ON PAGE 152)

(CONTINUED FROM PAGE 151)

FOR THE CAKE

1. Preheat the oven to 350°F (180°C, or gas mark 4) and grease and line two 6-inch (15-cm) cake tins with parchment paper.
2. Add the milk and lemon juice to a small bowl. Leave for 5 minutes to curdle.
3. To a large mixing bowl, add the softened butter and sugar. Using a handheld electric or freestanding mixer, beat for 1 to 2 minutes, until light and fluffy. Add the applesauce, vanilla, and the milk mixture. Beat again to fully combine. Do not worry if the mixture appears to split.
4. Sift the flour, baking powder, and baking soda into the bowl. Add the salt. Beat the mixture to reach a smooth cake batter with no specks of flour; do not overmix.
5. Fold in the chocolate chips and divide between the two tins. Smooth over the tops and bake for 25 to 27 minutes, or until an inserted skewer comes out clean. They will be golden and risen.
6. Cool for 10 minutes, then remove from the tins to cool fully on a wire rack.
7. To make the buttercream: Make up the vanilla buttercream and divide into two. To one half, add the chocolate chips. Place the second half in a piping bag with a star-shaped nozzle attached. Make up the chocolate buttercream.
8. If the cakes have domed, carefully slice off the tops to make the tops flat. Place one cake on a plate or cake stand and top with all of the chocolate chip–vanilla buttercream before sandwiching together with the second cake. Use the chocolate buttercream to cover all of the cake. I like to use an offset spatula for this.
9. Use the remaining vanilla buttercream to pipe on six swirls. Arrange some chocolate chip cookies on top.
10. Slice into the cake and enjoy. The cake will keep in the fridge, covered, for 3 to 5 days. Keep unfrosted cakes in the freezer, wrapped well, for up to 1 month; defrost at room temperature.

SERVING SUGGESTIONS AND VARIATIONS

- *These chocolate chip cookies are so delicious on their own, so you can bake up a batch to have with a coffee without having to make the cake, too.*
- *To keep this recipe gluten-free, make sure to use your favorite 1:1 gluten-free flour that contains xanthan gum.*

STRAWBERRIES-AND-CREAM CHEESECAKE

Serves: 10 to 12 | Time: 40 minutes plus overnight soaking and chilling

Brighten up your day with a slice of this berry-licious, no-bake cheesecake that is as light as clouds. It's smooth and creamy, packed with real strawberries, and hides a secret layer of strawberry chia jam. Made entirely from plant-based whole foods, this dessert is great topped with freshly whipped coconut cream and extra berries. You can make this ahead of time—the cheesecake keeps well in the fridge or freezer.

For the Strawberry Jam
- 1⅓ cups (200 g) fresh strawberries
- 2 tablespoons (30 ml) maple syrup
- ½ teaspoon vanilla extract
- 1 tablespoon (11 g) chia seeds

For the Base
- 10 pitted dates (1 packed cup, or 200 grams)
- 3 cups (300 g) oats
- ¾ cup (100 g) almonds
- ¼ cup (59 ml) melted coconut oil
- 1 teaspoon vanilla extract
- 1 tablespoon (15 ml) reserved date water

For the Cheesecake
- 1⅛ cup (158 g) cashews
- ½ cup (120 g) thick coconut yogurt or coconut cream
- ¼ cup (59 ml) melted coconut oil
- 2 tablespoons (30 ml) maple syrup
- 1 tablespoon (15 ml) lemon juice
- 5½ ounces (155 g) fresh strawberries (trimmed weight)
- 1½ tablespoons (9 g) strawberry powder (optional)

For Topping
- ¼ cup (60 g) thick coconut yogurt or cream
- Fresh strawberries

1. Soak the cashews for the filling: Add the cashews to a large bowl. Submerge with cold water and leave slightly covered overnight, or cover them in boiling water and soak for 1 hour. Grease a loose-bottomed 8-inch (20-cm) round cake tin.
2. To make the jam: Trim the strawberries and roughly chop them. Add them to a small saucepan with the maple syrup and vanilla. Bring to a boil, then simmer over medium heat for 10 minutes, stirring often to mash the berries. Stir in the chia seeds and pour into a blender. Blitz until mostly smooth. Pour into a small bowl and chill in the fridge where it will also thicken.
3. To make the base: Soak the dates in boiling water for 10 minutes. Drain, saving some of the water. Add the oats and almonds to a food processor and blitz to a fine meal. Add the soaked dates, coconut oil, and vanilla. Pulse to reach a sticky mix, scraping down the sides as needed. Add 1 tablespoon (15 ml) of date water as needed so the mixture sticks between your fingers. Press the base mix into the tin, saving two spoonfuls for the top. Press down firmly to make an even base and work your way up the sides to make a compact cheesecake case. Spread the base with half of the jam, and return it to the fridge.
4. To make the cheesecake filling: Drain and rinse the cashews and add to a high-speed blender with all the other ingredients. Blend until really creamy and no lumps remain. Pour the cheesecake into the base and smooth over the top. Tap the dish on the surface a couple of times to remove any air bubbles.

(CONTINUED ON PAGE 155)

(CONTINUED FROM PAGE 153)

5. Drop spoonfuls of the remaining strawberry jam and swirl the jam through using a knife. Allow to set in the fridge for 4 to 6 hours or overnight, until firm to touch.

6. To serve: Whip the yogurt until fluffy. Spoon it over the top, and add fresh strawberries along with the leftover biscuity base.

7. Cover the cheesecake and keep in the fridge for up to 1 week or in the freezer for up to 1 month.

SERVING SUGGESTIONS AND VARIATIONS

- *Keep this cheesecake gluten-free by making sure your oats are gluten-free*
- *This is a great dessert to make ahead and can be served from the freezer. Allow the cheesecake to thaw for 20 minutes before slicing for a firmer cheesecake experience.*

APPLE-AND-BLACKBERRY CRUMBLE PIE

Serves: 6 | Time: 60 minutes plus chilling

This dessert was a beautiful moment of indecision between pie and crumble, so I thought "why not have both?" It's a golden, flaky pastry with a sticky, fruity filling piled high with an oaty, crumbly mixture. While the pastry uses regular flour, the crumble has a more wholesome twist using oats and oat flour to make for the most delicious dessert. I love this warm with scoops of dairy-free ice cream, such as my Salted Caramel–Cookie Dough Ice Cream (page 159) or cold with spoonfuls of coconut yogurt.

For the Pastry
- 1½ cups (210 g) all-purpose flour or gluten-free flour, plus extra for dusting
- 3 tablespoons (36 g) caster sugar
- A pinch of salt
- ½ scant cup (100 g) vegan butter, cold*
- 2 tablespoons (28 ml) cold water

For the Filling
- 2 apples (peeled and cored: 7 ounces, or 200 g)
- 1 cup (140 g) blackberries
- ¼ cup (40 g) light brown sugar
- 1 tablespoon (8 g) cornstarch
- 1 tablespoon (15 ml) lemon juice
- 1 teaspoon ground cinnamon
- A pinch of salt

For the Crumble
- 1 cup (100 g) oat flour
- ½ cup (50 g) rolled oats
- 3 tablespoons (30 g) light brown sugar
- A pinch of salt
- 3 tablespoons (42 g) melted vegan butter

To Serve
- Dairy-free, vanilla ice cream

1. To make the pastry: Add the flour, sugar, and salt to a food processor. Pulse to combine. Add the cubed butter and continue to pulse to reach a fine crumble mix, then gradually pour in the cold water to form a ball of dough. Or, if using your hands, add the flour, sugar, and salt to a large bowl and mix. Add the butter and rub the mixture between your fingers to reach a fine crumble. Gradually stir in the water to reach a ball of dough. Wrap the dough tightly and chill in the fridge for 30 minutes.
2. Meanwhile, make the filling: Slice the apples into small cubes. Add to a large bowl with the rest of the filling ingredients. Toss well, and set it to one side.
3. To make the crumble topping: Stir together the oat flour, oats, sugar, and salt in a medium bowl. Pour over the melted butter, and stir to a sticky crumbly mix that clumps together.
4. When the pastry has rested, preheat the oven to 350°F (180°C, or gas mark 4) and grease and 8-inch (20-cm) pie dish with vegan butter.
5. Roll out the pastry on a lightly floured surface using a floured rolling pin, to ¼-inch (½-cm thick), to a circle that is larger than your dish. Carefully lift the pastry into the dish and press the pastry down. Trim the edges, leave a 1-inch (2½-cm) border. Fold this border of pastry down toward the outer edge of the dish and crimp all along the sides using your forefinger. The extra border of pastry strengthens the crimp, so it holds the shape better.
6. Prick the base all over with a fork, lay over a sheet of parchment and fill with baking beans. Blind bake for 15 minutes, then remove the pastry from the oven.

(CONTINUED ON PAGE 158)

(CONTINUED FROM PAGE 157)

7. Remove the baking beans and parchment paper. Pour in the filling with all the juices. Press down evenly, then cover with the crumble topping. Bake the crumble pie for 25 minutes. Cover with foil and bake for 10 minutes, until golden brown and bubbling at the edges.

8. Allow to rest for 5 minutes. Serve—warm or cool—with ice cream. Leftovers will keep in the fridge, covered, for 2 to 3 days or in the freezer for 2 to 4 weeks.

SERVING SUGGESTIONS AND VARIATIONS

* *For the butter, if using cups, measure ½ cup then remove 1 tablespoon.*

• *Why not try this crumble pie with other berries, such as raspberries or blueberries. Enjoy whatever is in season.*

SALTED CARAMEL–COOKIE DOUGH ICE CREAM

Serves: 8 | Time: 30 minutes plus chilling and freezing time, plus overnight soak

This ice cream is a pure joy to eat on a hot summer's day. It's thick, creamy, luscious, and packed with salty-sweet flavors. The best part is that this recipe is no-churn so there is no ice cream machine involved. You will need a high-speed blender and some patience to let the ice cream set—then you are ready to scoop away. Packed with gooey, homemade, salted caramel and chunks of edible cookie dough, serve this in bowls, in ice cream cones, or on top of Fudgy Raspberry Brownies (page 139).

For the Salted Caramel
- ½ batch of Salted Caramel (page 149 [Banoffee Pie Jars])

For the Cookie Dough
- ¼ cup (60 g) peanut butter
- 2 tablespoons (30 ml) maple syrup
- 1 teaspoon vanilla extract
- ½ cup (50 g) oat flour
- A pinch of salt
- 2 ounces (55 g) dairy-free chocolate chips

For the Ice Cream
- 1 cup (140 g) cashews
- 1 can (14 ounces, or 400 ml) full-fat coconut milk
- ⅔ cup (160 g) thick coconut yogurt or coconut cream*
- ¾ cup (180 ml) maple syrup
- 1½ tablespoons (25 ml) vanilla extract
- A pinch of salt

1. Prepare the salted caramel. Allow it to cool until ready to use; it does not have to be fully cool.
2. To make the cookie dough: In a large bowl, stir together the peanut butter, maple syrup, and vanilla until smooth. Add the oat flour and salt. Stir to a sticky dough. Fold in the chocolate chips and divide into small balls (using 1-teaspoon measure). Chill in the fridge until ready to use.
3. Add the cashews to a large bowl. Either cover with water and let them soak overnight (covered), or cover with boiling water and soak for 1 hour. Drain and rinse the cashews.
4. To make the ice cream: Add the drained cashews and all the ingredients to a high-speed blender or food processor. Blend until really smooth. Scrape down the sides as necessary and continue until no lumps remain.
5. Line a loaf pan with parchment paper so it overhangs the edges. Pour in the ice cream and cover tightly with plastic wrap. Place flat in the freezer for 1 hour.
6. Stir the ice cream and freeze for 30 minutes. The stirring process allows the ice cream to set evenly for the creamiest results.

(CONTINUED ON PAGE 161)

(CONTINUED FROM PAGE 159)

7. Add most the caramel in small spoonfuls and drop in most of the cookie dough pieces. Use a knife to swirl the caramel through the ice cream. Cover and freeze for 30 minutes. The mixture will be thicker, add the remaining caramel and cookie dough and double wrap in plastic wrap (to avoid ice forming on top). Carefully place in the freezer to set for 4 to 6 hours or overnight. Adding the fillings into two stages means every mouthful has caramel and cookie dough; it won't all sink to the bottom.

8. Allow the ice cream to thaw for 20 minutes at room temperature before scooping and enjoying. Store leftovers wrapped tightly in the freezer for 1 month.

SERVING SUGGESTIONS AND VARIATIONS

• *Make the caramel and cookie dough a few days in advance, as needed, as they will last for up to 1 week in sealed containers in the fridge.*

* *Coconut cream is the thick part of coconut milk. Place a can of full-fat coconut milk in the fridge overnight, then scoop off the solid cream part.*

7
CELEBRATIONS

From birthday parties to Easter get-togethers, Thanksgiving celebrations, and Christmastime dinners, this chapter has a range of recipes to make any gathering delicious. These crowd-pleasing recipes are just what you need to serve to friends and family to make every occasion that little bit more special. Indeed, some of these recipes have become new family favorites that we make time and time again.

With delicious sides and starters, hearty and wholesome main dishes, and showstopper desserts, these recipes have been created with love that you can pass on to your guests. The best way to anyone's heart is through their stomach!

Whether you are welcoming vegans, non-vegans, or flexitarians into your home, there is something for everyone. Fool everyone into thinking there's actual cheese in my ultimate Easy Vegan Cheesy Scalloped Potatoes (page 167), and wow guests with the Garlic-Tahini Whole Roasted Cauliflower (page 177). A lot of the recipes such as the Filo Pastry Parcels with Mushroom Gravy (page 171) can be made in advance so you can be the hostess with the most-ess.

KALE, POMEGRANATE, AND ALMOND WINTER SALAD

Serves: 4 | Time: 10 minutes

This kale salad is seriously craveable and one that the whole family will enjoy. The key to any good kale salad is to massage your leaves. This wilts the leaves, turning them vibrant green and making them much more enjoyable as a base for this wintery, slaw-style salad. Add some dried cranberries, fresh pomegranate, and crunchy slivered almonds for a festive side dish.

For the Dressing
- ¼ cup (60 ml) orange juice
- 1 tablespoon (15 ml) olive oil
- 1 tablespoon (15 ml) apple cider vinegar
- 1 teaspoon maple syrup
- ½–1 teaspoon Dijon mustard
- Salt and pepper, to taste

For the Salad
- 2 cups (4 big leaves) chopped lacinato kale
- 1 cup (100 g) shredded white cabbage
- 1 cup (100 g) shredded red cabbage
- 2 scallions, sliced
- 1 apple, thinly sliced
- ½ cup (60 g) dried cranberries
- ½ cup (50 g) pomegranate, plus extra for serving
- 2 satsumas, peeled and sliced
- ½ cup (40 g) slivered almonds, plus extra for serving

1. To make the dressing: Add all of the ingredients to a jar and seal the lid. Shake well to emulsify the dressing. Alternatively, stir together in a small bowl. Season with salt and pepper.
2. To make the salad: Add the kale to a large bowl with a pinch of salt. Massage with your hands for 1 minute to wilt the leaves. Stir in the white and red cabbage, and massage together with half of the dressing.
3. Add the apple, dried cranberries, pomegranate, satsumas, and almonds to the salad with the rest of the dressing. Toss well.
4. Serve topped with extra pomegranate and almonds. Enjoy right away or keep in a sealed container in the fridge for 2 to 3 days.

SERVING SUGGESTIONS AND VARIATIONS
- *This is a great salad to make for potlucks, picnics, and other gatherings. Or make it up and add it to a Nourish Bowl (page 94).*
- *To keep this salad nut-free, omit the almonds and swap for seeds such as sunflower or pumpkin seeds.*

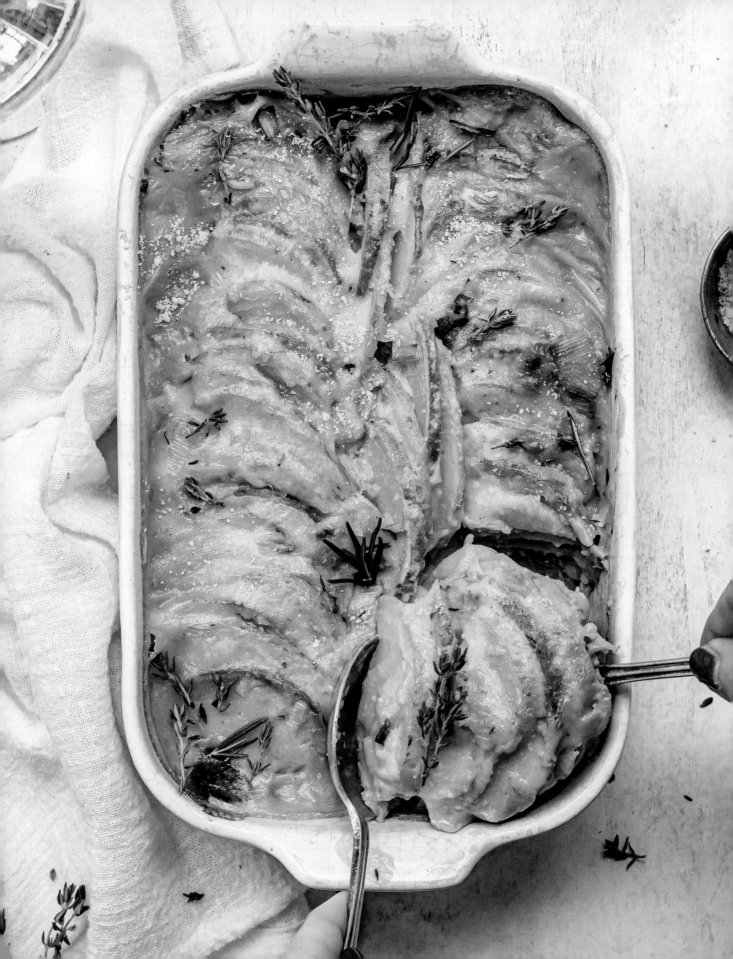

EASY VEGAN CHEESY
SCALLOPED POTATOES

Serves: 4 | Time: 75 minutes

These potatoes are pure comfort in every mouthful. They are warming, tender, slightly crisp on top and oh-so-cheesy (without any cheese). These scalloped potatoes get their rich flavor from a quick vegan parmesan, and they will take your roast dinner to the next level.

**For the Homemade
Vegan Parmesan**
- ½ cup (70 g) cashews
- 3 tablespoons (15 g) nutritional yeast
- Salt

For the Potatoes
- 1½ lb. (700 g) potatoes (I use 2 sweet and 2 regular potatoes.)
- 2 tablespoons (30 ml) olive oil
- 1 leek, chopped small
- 4 cloves garlic, crushed
- 2 tablespoons (16 g) cornstarch
- 1½ cups (360 ml) unsweetened plant-based milk
- ½ cup (120 ml) vegetable broth or stock
- ¼ teaspoon hot smoked paprika
- A pinch of ground turmeric (for color; optional)
- ¼ cup Homemade Vegan Parmesan, as above
- Salt and pepper, to taste
- Fresh herbs, such as thyme and rosemary, to garnish

1. To make the parmesan: Blitz together the ingredients in a small blender or food processor. Set it aside.
2. Preheat the oven to 350°F (180°C, or gas mark 4) and have a dish to hand.
3. Either peel the potatoes or leave the skin on; I love the texture that the skin adds. Evenly and thinly slice the potatoes; this ensures they will cook evenly.
4. Heat the olive oil in a large frying pan. Once hot, add the leek and garlic. Fry for 5 minutes, until softening and fragrant. Use a balloon whisk to stir in the cornstarch.
5. Slowly and gradually, pour in the milk while whisking continuing to make a smooth sauce with no lumps. Continue to use all the milk, then whisk in the broth. Once fully combined, allow to bubble over high heat for 5 minutes, whisking well until thick.
6. Pour the sauce into a blender with the hot smoked paprika, turmeric (if using), and vegan parmesan. Season with salt and pepper. Blend until thick and creamy.
7. Arrange the potatoes in a dish; mine is 6 x 9 inches (15 x 23 cm). Make sure they overlap and are nestled in tightly. Alternate between sweet and regular potatoes, if you like. Pour over the sauce.
8. Bake for 25 minutes. Cover with foil and bake for 30 to 35 minutes, until golden and crisp on top, bubbling at the sides, and the potatoes are tender.
9. Serve warm, topped with herbs and parmesan. Once cold, leftovers will keep in a sealed container in the fridge for 2 to 3 days. Store extra parmesan in an airtight container for 2 to 3 weeks.

SERVING SUGGESTIONS AND VARIATIONS
Make these potatoes nut-free by using a nut-free milk and swap the cashews in the parmesan for sunflowers seeds.

CELEBRATIONS SHARING SNACK BOARD

Serves: 4 to 6 | Time: 10 minutes

Snack boards, charcuterie boards, sharing boards . . . whatever you like to call them, these boards of snacks and mini bites are great for entertaining. Mix and match whatever you like on these boards and guests are sure to keep coming back for more.

Recipes Featured
- Creamy Hummus (page 69)
- Roasted Red Pepper Dip (page 79)
- Garlic-Herb Cashew Cheese (page 135)
- Sun-Dried Tomato and Olive Cheese Scones (page 133)
- Falafel Bites (page 69)
- Homemade Seedy Crackers (page 119)

Extras to Add
- Chopped cucumber
- Halved tomatoes
- Grapes
- Bowls of olives and sun-dried tomatoes

Other Ideas
- Two-Ingredient Flatbreads (page 121)
- Slices of Mixed Vegetable Frittata (page 77)
- Cashew-Cauliflower (page 105 [Cashew Cauliflower and Spinach Dahl])
- Other crudités, such as carrot sticks, bell pepper, etc.

1. To make the perfect savory snack board, have all of your components to hand so you can visualize how the board will come together.
2. Place some items in bowls, such as hummus and red pepper dip. Place the bowls and larger items, such as the cashew cheese and scones on the board first.
3. Add the medium-size components, such as falafel bites and seedy crackers.
4. Fill in the gaps with smaller bowls of olives, sun-dried tomatoes, and fresh cucumber, tomatoes, and grapes.
5. Depending on the components, boards can be prepared 1 to 2 hours in advance. Keep them covered in the fridge when needed.

SERVING SUGGESTIONS AND VARIATIONS
Remember that anything goes for a snack board. Just make sure there is a variety of color, flavor, and foods.

FILO PASTRY PARCELS
WITH MUSHROOM GRAVY

Serves: 6 | Time: 60 minutes

These filo parcels are the perfectly portioned to serve one roast dinner at a time to hungry guests. They are full of hearty and wholesome ingredients, warming roast flavors, and tons of vegetables. Serve them with plenty of my mushroom gravy (which I practically drink every time I make this recipe) and the delicious sticky roasted vegetables. All the effort is in the preparation for these parcels, meaning you can relax once everything is in the oven.

For the Easy Vegan Mushroom Gravy
- 2 tablespoons (30 ml) olive oil
- ½ white onion, small dice
- 3 cloves garlic, crushed
- 6 ounces (170 g) mushrooms, chopped small
- ½ teaspoon dried thyme
- ½ teaspoon dried rosemary
- 2 tablespoons (16 g) cornstarch
- 1⅔ cups (400 ml) vegetable stock or broth
- 1 tablespoon (15 ml) tamari
- Salt and pepper, to taste

For the Filo Parcels
- 3 tablespoons (45 ml) olive oil, divided
- 1 red onion, small dice
- 4 cloves garlic, crushed
- 7 ounces (200 g) mushrooms, chopped small
- 1½ cups (210 g) butternut squash, chopped small
- 1 teaspoon dried thyme
- 1 teaspoon dried rosemary
- 1 teaspoon dried sage
- Salt and pepper, to taste
- ¼ teaspoon ground nutmeg
- ½ heaped cup (100 g) precooked chestnuts, chopped
- ½ cup (100 g) dried apricots, chopped
- 1 can green lentils (drained: 8½ ounces, or 240 g)
- 2 tablespoons (28 ml) tamari
- 1 tablespoon (16 g) tomato purée
- 6 sheets of filo pastry

For the Sticky Roasted Carrots and Parsnips
- 2 large carrots, peeled (14 ounces, or 400 g)
- 2 large parsnips, peeled (14 ounces, or 400 g)
- 1½ teaspoons olive oil
- 1½ teaspoons maple syrup
- Salt and pepper, to taste

To Serve
- Extra vegetables, such as broccoli
- Homemade Cranberry Sauce (page 173)
- Easy Vegan Cheesy Scalloped Potatoes (page 167)

(CONTINUED ON PAGE 172)

(CONTINUED FROM PAGE 171)

1. To make the mushroom gravy: Heat the olive oil in a large pan over high heat. Once hot, add the onion, garlic, and mushrooms. Fry for 7 to 10 minutes, until the mushrooms are tender and have released their juices. Add the thyme and rosemary, and fry for 1 minute. Using a balloon whisk, pour in the cornstarch and stir to combine. Gradually pour in the stock while whisking the pan over high heat. Once all the stock has been added, allow the gravy to bubble, while stirring, for 3 minutes, until thicker. Pour the gravy into a blender with the tamari. Season with salt and pepper, and blend until creamy and smooth. Keep warm on the stove, or cool and store in a sealed container in the fridge for up to 3 days.

2. To make the filo parcel filling: Heat 2 tablespoons (30 ml) of olive oil in a large frying pan over high heat. Once hot, add the onion and garlic. Fry off for 5 minutes over high heat. Add the mushrooms and fry for 5 minutes, until the mushrooms are tender. Add the butternut squash, dried herbs, nutmeg, salt, and pepper. Cook for 5 minutes, to soften the squash.

3. To the pan, add the chestnuts, apricots, lentils, tamari, and tomato purée. Stir everything well. Allow the mixture to cool while you prepare the carrots, or store it in the fridge for up to 3 days.

4. Preheat the oven to 350°F (180°C, or gas mark 4). Line a large pan with parchment or tinfoil. Slice the carrots and parsnips into batons, all about the same size. Add them to the pan and toss with the olive oil, maple syrup, salt, and pepper. Bake for 40 minutes, until they are tender and sticky, turning halfway through.

5. Meanwhile, make the parcels: Work in batches, so the pastry does not dry out and keep extra pastry under a tea towel. Slice one sheet of pastry in half to make two squares. Brush one lightly with the extra 1 tablespoon (15 ml) of olive oil and place the second sheet on top at an angle to make a star-shape. Lightly brush the edges with oil. Place a heaped ½ cup (150 to 160 g) of the filling in the center and shape into a circle. Use your hands to carefully fold edges of the pastry up toward the center and secure with some cooking string or twist well. Repeat to make six parcels and brush them all the oil.

6. Bake the parcels for 20 to 25 minutes, until golden and crisp. Cover the tops of the parcels with tinfoil if they are browning too quickly.

7. Serve the filo parcels alongside the roasted vegetables and the gravy as well as any other vegetables and some cranberry sauce.

SERVING SUGGESTIONS AND VARIATIONS

- *These parcels will keep well in the fridge for 2 to 3 days. The filling can be prepared a few days before, too.*
- *To make these gluten-free, make sure your filo pastry is gluten-free. Swap the chestnuts for seeds to make these parcels nut-free.*

NUT ROAST WITH MAPLE-PECAN SPROUTS AND CRANBERRY SAUCE

Serves: 6 to 8 | Time: 20 minutes prep plus 60 minutes cooking

This nut roast is much lighter on the nuts than most, and that is just how I like it. Instead, it is packed with a range of vegetables, lots of fresh herbs, dried cranberries as well as the roasted chestnuts and cashews to make a truly delicious roast diner main course for all the family. I cannot count the number of times I've eaten nut roast while developing this recipe, but I am not mad about it! Plus, the maple-pecan sprouts are seriously addicting—even sprout haters will be tempted.

For the Nut Roast

- ½ cup plus 2 tablespoons (101 g) dry quinoa or bulgur wheat
- 2 medium parsnips, peeled and chopped (8 ounces, or 220 g)
- 2 tablespoons (18 g) ground chia or flaxseed, plus 5 tablespoon (74 ml) water
- 2 tablespoons (30 ml) olive oil
- 1 red onion, small dice
- 4 cloves garlic, crushed
- 11 ounces (310 g) mushrooms, chopped very small
- 4 sprigs fresh rosemary or 1 teaspoon dried rosemary
- 4 sprigs fresh thyme or 1 teaspoon dried thyme
- ¼ teaspoon ground nutmeg
- ½ cup (70 g) cashews, chopped small
- ½ heaped cup (100 g) precooked chestnuts, chopped small
- ½ cup (70 g) dried cranberries
- ¼ cup (60 ml) tamari
- Salt and pepper, to taste

For the Sticky Maple Sprouts

- 4½ cups (400 g) Brussel sprouts (peeled and trimmed weight)
- 2 red onions
- 2 tablespoons (30 ml) olive oil
- 2 tablespoons (30 ml) maple syrup
- 1 teaspoon tamari
- ½ cup (60 g) pecans
- Salt and pepper, to taste

For the Cranberry Sauce

- 1 large orange, zested and juiced
- 4 cups (400 g) fresh cranberries
- ¼ cup (60 ml) maple syrup
- A pinch of nutmeg

To Serve

- Easy Vegan Mushroom Gravy (page 171)
- Easy Vegan Cheesy Scalloped Potatoes (page 167)

1. Preheat the oven the 400°F (200°C, or gas mark 6). Line a loaf pan with parchment paper.
2. Cook the quinoa according to package instructions and set it to one side. At the same time, boil or steam the parsnips until soft. Drain the parsnips. Mash them in a large mixing bowl until smooth.
3. Stir together the chia seeds with water and leave for 5 minutes to form a gel.
4. Heat the olive oil in a large frying pan. Add the onion and garlic with a pinch of salt. Fry for 5 minutes, until softening. Add the mushrooms and fry for 5 minutes, so they release their juices. Add the herbs and nutmeg. Fry for 1 minute, until fragrant. Toss in the cashews, chestnuts, and cranberries.

(CONTINUED ON PAGE 175)

(CONTINUED FROM PAGE 173)

5. Pour the mushroom mix into the parsnips along with the cooked quinoa, chia gel, and tamari. Season with salt and pepper. Give the mixture a very good stir so the chia gel disperses evenly.

6. Transfer the mixture to the lined pan and press down firmly to make the nut roast compact. Bake for 35 minutes. Cover with tinfoil and bake for 20 minutes, until crisp on top and firm to touch.

7. Meanwhile, make the sides: Slice the spouts in half and the onions into chunks. Add to a large, lined baking sheet. Toss with the olive oil, maple syrup, tamari, and pecans. Season with salt and pepper. Bake alongside the nut roast for 30 to 40 minutes, or until tender and crisping at the edges.

8. At the same time, cook the cranberry sauce (this can be done up to 1 week ahead of time). Measure out ½ cup (120 ml) of orange juice. To a saucepan, add the cranberries, orange zest, orange juice, maple syrup, and nutmeg. Stir well, bring to the boil and simmer and bubble over medium heat for 15 to 20 minutes, or until thick and glossy. While cooking, stir the pot and break down the berries with the spoon. The sauce will thicken as it cools. Once cool, pour into a container and cover.

9. When the nut roast is cooked, allow it to cool for 10 minutes in the pan before lifting out and slicing with a large knife. Serve alongside the sprouts, cranberry sauce, some gravy, and potatoes.

SERVING SUGGESTIONS AND VARIATIONS

- *This roast is great to make ahead of time. Once cooled, wrap tightly and keep in the fridge for 3 to 5 days or in the freezer for up to 1 month. I like to slice it once cool and wrap up slices individually to enjoy later. Defrost at room temperature and warm back up in the oven.*

- *To make this nut roast nut-free, swap the cashews and chestnuts for seeds, such as sunflower and pumpkin seeds.*

- *For the neatest slices, slice the nut roast once cool and make sure the vegetables and nuts are chopped small when they go into the mix.*

GARLIC-TAHINI WHOLE ROASTED CAULIFLOWER

Serves: 4 | Time: 1 hour 15 minutes

I never thought I'd see the day when my family would thoroughly enjoy cauliflower, but this recipe proves me wrong. Tender on the inside and crispy golden outside, this garlicky and tahini-covered cauliflower is baked alongside crispy cauliflower leaves—one of my best no-waste tricks! It's served with creamy hummus for the most delicious and show-stopping centerpiece. It's easy to make, naturally gluten-free, and a real crowd pleaser.

For the Marinade
- 1 medium cauliflower
- 2 tablespoons (15 g) runny tahini
- 2 tablespoons (30 ml) olive oil
- 2 tablespoons (28 ml) lemon juice
- 2 tablespoons (28 ml) water
- ½ teaspoon miso paste or 1 teaspoon tamari
- 3 large cloves garlic, crushed
- Salt and pepper, to taste

For the Dressing
- ½ cup (120 g) coconut yogurt
- 1½ teaspoons lemon juice
- 1 teaspoon apple cider vinegar

To Serve
- 1 tablespoon (15 ml) olive oil
- 1 cup (246 g) Hummus (page 69)
- 2 tablespoons (18 g) Dukkah (page 97) or chopped nuts
- 1 tablespoon (about 6 g) chopped fresh herbs, such as mint, parsley, or cilantro
- ¼ cup (45 g) pomegranate

1. To make the cauliflower: Trim the base and the leaves off the cauliflower head and keep the leaves to one side. Stir together all the ingredients for the marinade in a large mixing bowl. Transfer the cauliflower to the bowl. Use your hands to rub the marinade all over, working into the base, too. Leave for 10 minutes or up to 2 hours.
2. When ready to cook the cauliflower, preheat the oven to 350°F (180°C, or gas mark 4). Place the cauliflower in the middle of a baking dish, rubbing any leftover marinade into the vegetable, saving 1 tablespoon (15 ml) of marinade for later.
3. Bake for 30 minutes. Cover with tinfoil and bake for 20 to 30 minutes, or until tender inside and crisping and golden outside.
4. Meanwhile, make the dressing: In a small bowl, stir together all the ingredients with the reserved marinade until smooth and creamy. Add water as needed for a pourable consistency.
5. Prepare the hummus, dukkah, and fresh herbs.
6. Line a tray with parchment paper. With 10 minutes left of baking time, rub the 1 tablespoon (15 ml) of olive oil into the cauliflower leaves and season with salt and paper. Bake on the tray for 10 minutes, turning over halfway through until crisp.
7. To serve: Spread the hummus on a large plate, top with the baked whole roasted cauliflower and the cauliflower leaf crisps. Drizzle over the yogurt dressing. Sprinkle with the dukkah, herbs, and pomegranate.

SERVING SUGGESTIONS AND VARIATIONS
- *Try serving whole roasted cauliflower alongside the Kale, Pomegranate, and Almond Winter Salad (page 165) and Easy Vegan Cheesy Scalloped Potatoes (page 167).*
- *Got any leftovers? Once cold, this is equally delicious in lunch boxes the next day.*

PUMPKIN SPICE LAYER CAKE

Serves: 8 to 10 | Time: 50 minutes plus cooling

This cake reminds me of Cinderella's fairy godmother turning a pumpkin into a carriage. . . . well, how about turning it into this amazing two-tier layer cake filled with fluffy vanilla buttercream! Decorated with easy buttercream pumpkins, it is the best and most delicious festive cake.

For the Cake
- 1⅓ cups (320 ml) plant-based milk
- 2 tablespoons (28 ml) lemon juice
- ⅔ cup (150 g) pumpkin purée
- 1 cup (160 g) coconut sugar
- 2 teaspoons (10 ml) vanilla extract
- 1½ cups (210 g) all-purpose flour
- 2 teaspoons (5 g) ground cinnamon
- 1 teaspoon ground ginger
- ½ teaspoon mixed spice
- ¼ teaspoon ground cloves
- 1½ teaspoons baking soda
- ½ teaspoon baking powder
- A pinch of salt

For the Orange and Green Buttercream
- ¼ cup (56 g) vegan butter, softened
- ¾ cup (120 g) confectioners' sugar
- 1 teaspoon plant-based milk
- ½ teaspoon vanilla extract
- Orange food gel
- Green food gel

For the White Buttercream
- ⅓ cup (76 g) vegan butter, softened
- 1½ cups (240 g) confectioners' sugar
- 1½ tablespoons (25 ml) plant-based milk
- 1 teaspoon vanilla extract
- Sprinkles

1. Preheat the oven to 350°F (180°C, or gas mark 4). Grease and line two 6-inch (15-cm) round cake tins with parchment paper.
2. Stir together the milk and lemon juice, and leave it for 5 minutes to curdle. Whisk in the pumpkin purée, coconut sugar, and vanilla.
3. Sift in the remaining ingredients. Add the salt and whisk again until no specks of flour remain.
4. Divide the batter evenly between the two cake tins and bake for 35 to 40 minutes, or until an inserted skewer comes out clean.
5. Let the cakes cool for 10 minutes. Carefully remove them from the tins to cool fully on a wire rack. Once cool, slice off the tops to make them flat, if necessary.
6. To make the colored buttercream: Beat the butter with an electric freestanding or handheld mixer until fluffy. Gradually beat in the confectioners' sugar, milk, and vanilla. Color three-quarters of the mixture with 1 to 2 drops of orange food gel and remaining one-quarter with 1 to 2 drops of green food gel.
7. Transfer the buttercreams to two separate piping bags; a star-shaped nozzle for the orange and a small round one for the green.

(CONTINUED ON PAGE 180)

(CONTINUED FROM PAGE 179)

8. To make the white buttercream: Repeat step 6.
9. Add one cake to a plate and add some white buttercream. Top it with the second cake, and cover the sides and top with the rest of the white buttercream. Chill in the fridge for 10 minutes to set.
10. Pipe on orange buttercream pumpkins around the base of the cake and add green stalks. Use extra buttercream for a pumpkin patch on top. Add the sprinkles.
11. Chill for 10 minutes before slicing. Store leftovers in the fridge for 3 to 5 days; unfrosted cakes will keep in the freezer for 1 month.

GINGERBREAD LAYER CAKE WITH GINGERBREAD COOKIES

Serves: 8 to 10 | Time: 60 minutes plus cooling

Christmastime will always bring with it a ton of gingerbread. This layer cake takes everything I love about gingerbread cookies and combines it with deliciously moist, fluffy, and spiced sponges. Spread thickly with luscious vanilla buttercream, this is one-layer cake that my family love at Christmastime—and all year long!

For the Gingerbread Cookies

- ¼ cup (56 g) vegan butter
- ¼ cup plus 2 tablespoons (75 g) caster sugar
- 2 tablespoons (30 ml) molasses
- 3 tablespoons (45 g) applesauce
- 1¼ cups (175 g) all-purpose flour
- ½ teaspoon ground ginger
- ½ teaspoon ground cinnamon
- A pinch of salt
- 1 cup (120 g) confectioners' sugar
- 1 tablespoon (15 ml) water

For the Gingerbread Layer Cake

- 1 cup plus 2 tablespoons (270 ml) plant-based milk
- 1½ teaspoons lemon juice
- ¼ cup plus 2 tablespoons (90 ml) sunflower oil
- 1½ teaspoons molasses
- ½ cup plus 2 tablespoons (120 g) caster sugar
- 3 tablespoons (30 g) light brown sugar
- 1½ tablespoons (25 ml) vanilla extract
- 2¼ cups (315 g) self-raising flour
- ¾ teaspoon baking powder
- ¾ teaspoon baking soda
- 1½ teaspoons ground ginger
- 1½ teaspoons ground cinnamon
- ½ teaspoon nutmeg
- A pinch of salt
- Cranberries
- Redcurrants
- Rosemary
- Sprinkles

For the Buttercream

- ½ cup (115 g) vegan butter
- 2 cups (320 g) confectioners' sugar
- 2 tablespoons (28 ml) plant-based milk
- 1 teaspoon vanilla extract

TO MAKE THE GINGERBREAD COOKIES

1. Beat together the butter and sugar until smooth. Beat in the molasses and applesauce; the mixture may split but this is okay. Beat in the flour, ginger, cinnamon, and salt. Continue to reach a smooth, sticky cookie dough. Shape into a ball and wrap in plastic wrap. Chill for 30 minutes in the fridge.
2. Preheat the oven to 350°F (180°C, or gas mark 4). Line three baking sheets with parchment.

(CONTINUED ON PAGE 183)

(CONTINUED FROM PAGE 181)

3. On a floured surface, roll out the gingerbread dough to ½-inch (1-cm) thick and cut out shapes. Reroll the scraps as necessary to use all the dough. Transfer the cookies to the baking sheets and bake one sheet at a time for 7 to 8 minutes. Keep the cut-out cookies in the fridge before baking to retain their shape once baked.

4. Cool the cookies on a wire rack fully. To decorate, stir the confectioners' sugar and water together until thick and transfer to a piping bag. Snip off the end and decorate the cookies.

5. Cookies will keep in a sealed container at room temperature for 1 to 2 weeks.

FOR THE GINGERBREAD LAYER CAKE

1. Preheat the oven to 350°F (180°C, or gas mark 4). Grease and line three 6-inch (15-cm) round cake tins.

2. Whisk together the milk and lemon juice in a large mixing bowl. Leave it for 5 minutes to curdle. Whisk in the sunflower oil, molasses, both sugars, and vanilla until smooth.

3. Sift in the flour, baking powder, baking soda, ginger, cinnamon, and nutmeg. Add the salt. Whisk until no specks of flour remain and the batter is smooth.

4. Divide between the three tins, and smooth over the tops. Bake for 20 to 22 minutes, or until an inserted skewer comes out clean. Cool for 10 minutes, then carefully remove from the tins to cool fully on a wire rack.

5. When ready, make the buttercream: Beat the softened butter until smooth. Gradually beat in the confectioners' sugar, milk, and vanilla. Continue to beat for 1 to 2 minutes, until fluffy.

6. Slice off the top of the cakes if they have rounded to make the tops even. Place a smear of buttercream on a serving plate and place on one cake. Spread with some of the buttercream, add the second cake, and repeat to top with the third cake. Use a tilted spatula to evenly coat the cake with the buttercream over the sides and the top.

7. Chill the cake in the fridge for 10 minutes to set the frosting. Decorate with any leftover buttercream to make Christmas trees. Add some gingerbread cookies, rosemary for trees, cranberries, redcurrants, and sprinkles. Dust with confectioners' sugar.

8. Slice and enjoy the cake, or keep covered in the fridge for 3 to 5 days. Best enjoyed at room temperature. Unfrosted cakes will keep for 1 month in the freezer.

SERVING SUGGESTIONS AND VARIATIONS

Make this cake into two 8-inch (20-cm) cake tins; the cakes will need slightly longer to bake. You also can make this into a smaller cake by dividing the cake by three to make a one-layer cake or make two-thirds of the batter to make two 6-inch (15-cm) cakes.

RED VELVET CUPCAKES WITH CHOCOLATE-VANILLA SWIRL BUTTERCREAM

Serves: 12 | Time: 30 minutes plus cooling

I had a lot of fun working on these cupcakes, and I licked many bowls of batter and buttercream in the process. These cupcakes may stray slightly from the traditional cream cheese frosting, but this easy chocolate-vanilla swirl buttercream takes these vegan, fluffy, and delicious red velvet cupcakes to the next level. Plus, they have a two-ingredient chocolate ganache middle . . . pure bliss in cupcake form!

For the Cupcakes
- ¾ cup plus 1 tablespoon (200 ml) plant-based milk
- 1 tablespoon (15 ml) lemon juice or apple cider vinegar
- ¼ cup (60 ml) sunflower oil
- ½ cup (100 g) applesauce
- ½ cup (100 g) caster sugar
- 1½ teaspoons vanilla extract
- 1½ cups (210 g) all-purpose flour
- 2 teaspoons (6 g) cornstarch
- 2 scant tablespoons (9 g) cacao powder
- 1 teaspoon baking powder
- ½ teaspoon baking soda
- A pinch of salt
- 7–8 drops red food gel

For the Chocolate Ganache
- 2 ounces (56 g) dark chocolate
- ¼ cup (60 ml) full-fat coconut milk

For the Chocolate Buttercream
- ¼ cup (56 g) vegan butter, softened
- 1 cup (100 g) confectioners' sugar
- 3 tablespoons (16 g) cacao powder
- 2 tablespoons (30 ml) aquafaba or plant-based milk

For the Vanilla Buttercream
- ¼ cup (56 g) vegan butter
- 1½ cups (150 g) confectioners' sugar
- 1–2 tablespoons (15–30 ml) aquafaba or plant-based milk
- ½ teaspoon vanilla extract

1. Preheat the oven to 350°F (180°C, or gas mark 4). Line twelve cupcake holes with cases.
2. Add the milk and lemon juice to a large mixing bowl and whisk. Leave for 5 minutes to curdle.
3. Whisk in the sunflower oil, applesauce, caster sugar, and vanilla.
4. Sift in the flour, cornstarch, cacao powder, baking powder, and baking soda. Add the salt and whisk until almost smooth. Add the red food gel and continue to whisk until no lumps remain.
5. Use an ice cream scoop or large tablespoon measure to divide the batter between the twelve cases, filling about two-thirds full. Bake for 15 to 16 minutes, until an inserted skewer comes out clean.
6. Remove carefully from the oven and transfer to a cooling rack to cool fully.

(CONTINUED ON PAGE 186)

(CONTINUED FROM PAGE 185)

7. Meanwhile, make the chocolate ganache: Chop the chocolate very small and pour into a heat-proof bowl. Warm the coconut milk until it just starts to bubble but do not let it boil. Pour over the chocolate and leave it for 5 minutes. Whisk the mixture until silky smooth. Allow the ganache to rest for 20 to 30 minutes, until thickened.

8. To make the buttercreams: In separate bowls for the vanilla and chocolate, beat the butter with an electric handheld or free-standing mixer until smooth. Gradually beat in the remaining ingredients until super light and fluffy.

9. Place the chocolate buttercream in one piping bag and the vanilla in a second piping bag. Cut off the ends, then place both inside a third piping bag with a star-shaped nozzle attached.

10. Core the middle of the cupcakes; crumble up this middle bit of cake to use for the topping. Pour in some chocolate ganache. Pipe on the swirl buttercream, then sprinkle with the cake crumbs and extra chocolate.

11. Enjoy the cupcakes right away, or keep in a sealed container in the fridge for 3 to 5 days. Unfrosted cupcakes can keep in the freezer for up to 1 month

NOTES:

- *The chocolate ganache is delicious to use on top of breakfast bowls, pancakes, and waffles, too. (See pages 15 and 37 [Breakfast and Brunch chapters])*
- *Check the red food gel is vegan. If needed, and add slightly more than you think as the batter will darken as it bakes.*

RESOURCES

Store-bought, plant-based options have come such a long way over the past few years. I'd love to give a shout-out to the brands that have helped make the recipes in this cookbook the most delicious they could ever be. Explore and experiment as you'd like!

Dairy-Free Alternatives
My go-to thick yogurt brand is Cocos Organic in the U.K.; in the U.S. I like CoYo, Kite Hill, or Chobani nondairy. I love Nush or Violife cream cheese; the cream cheese in the U.K. is slightly softer than U.S. varieties. For dairy-free butter, I love Naturli' in the U.K.; try Flora Plant-Based or Miyoko's Creamery for U.S. readers. There are too many nondairy milks to name; just choose your favorite one. For canned coconut milk and cream, my favorite brand is Nature's Charm which offers whipping cream and condensed milk, and it is available worldwide.

Pantry Staples
I get a lot of my pantry staples such as nuts, seeds, oats, and whole grains in bulk from KoRo. You'll be amazed at what's on offer at your local store or the zero-waste shops you can visit. For cans/tins of beans and pulses, for flour, baking essentials, and most other items, your local supermarket is your best friend for budget-friendly ingredients. A special mention to Nature's Heart, their raw cacao powder and cacao nibs are featured in this book.

Fruits and Vegetables
Eating seasonally and locally is the tastiest, most environmentally friendly, and least expensive way to enjoy food. Where the recipes offer swaps for fresh produce, use what you already have or buy what's in season. I love to visit the farmers' markets when I can, (which isn't too often where I live). Otherwise, I opt for supermarket produce with minimal packaging.

Chocolate
HU chocolate has just landed in the U.K. in the last year. I am in love with their simple ingredients, the rich favor, and the plastic-free packaging. I am also a huge fan of Divine Chocolate as well as supporting smaller, artisanal, plant-based chocolate brands.

ACKNOWLEDGMENTS

I am overwhelmed with gratitude for you holding this book in your hand, so firstly I want to thank you for picking up *Nourishing Vegan Every Day* to add to your cookbook collection. To everyone who has ever visited my website, and especially to those who have made a *Nourishing Amy* recipe, this book is because of you. This book would not have been possible without your continued support, recipe making, and feedback.

To my mum and dad, the biggest thank you goes to you. Thank you for supporting my dreams to work in the health and food scene (without knowing what the future would hold and if I could ever make a living out of it). Thank you for always being my rock, for listening to my endless chatter about cake batters, and for testing every single recipe that comes out of my kitchen. Thank you for giving me a loving home to pursue my career and for always encouraging me to be the best that I can be. I hope I have made you proud.

Thank you to my family and friends who have always believed in me. You have unknowingly tasted and given feedback on so many recipes in this book, and I would not have been able to build up the business without your similar passion for plant-based living and for delicious food. A special thank you to the very few people who knew about the book and were only too happy to be my baking guinea pigs!

A more unexpected thank you goes to the regular delivery drivers who drop parcels off at the doorstep. You have tried more recipes from my website and this book than you realize. To my lovely neighbors who gratefully accept all the cakes, pies, and cookies with which I turn up at your door; it's a joy to share them with you.

Finally, thank you to the wonderful team at Quarto Publishing; thank you for realizing my ambitions and putting my name on the front cover of a cookbook. Thank you to Thom for stumbling across my website, drawn in by a Vegan Black Forest Gateau I'd shared online. Connecting over cake felt like the best way to start working together, and it's been a pleasure to work with you. Thank you to Heather and your talented team for your immensely positive reaction to the imagery throughout the book and for bringing the book to life.

FOOD PHOTOGRAPHY

One of the key investments I made in my career was learning the art of food photography: a skill which I will forever continue to hone and perfect. I have learned so much from Sarah and her team at Foodtography School, whose online course I am enrolled in and have since moved on to the advanced course. We study the fundamentals of photography, principles of composition, the importance and qualities of light, creating your personal brand, editing essentials, the role of social media, and how to market to your audience and work with brands. Suffice to say, without the knowledge I gained from the school, you would not have this book in your hands. I have links on my website and social media for more information on the courses.

ABOUT THE AUTHOR

Amy Lanza is the plant-based recipe developer, food and content creator, food stylist, and photographer behind *Nourishing Amy.* She is passionate about food, health, and happiness, and she promotes a mindful balance in life. From kale salads to chocolate cake, there is room for it all. She focuses on vibrant, delicious, and easy vegan meals using seasonal and fresh ingredients for everyday healthy living. The word "nourish" embodies Amy's 360 holistic approach to well-being: health is not only the foods on our plate, but how we think, how we eat, and how we feel—though good food is the best place to start. Amy's work has been featured on the front covers of *Vegan Life* and *PlantBased* magazines. She has also been included in many other vegan publications, including *Thrive* and *Vegan Food and Living* magazine.

INDEX